HELL ON EARTH

David Bowen

Little Skye Publishing

HELL ON EARTH

Little Skye Publishing

In this work of fiction, the characters, places and events are either the product of the author's imagination or they are used entirely fictitiously.

Cover Illustration by Mick Minogue
Cover Design by Rueben Whitehouse

To Connie Bowen
for the endless support and
encouragement throughout my life.

And Laura Elizabeth Oliver
for the word groovy.

Acknowledgements

A big thankyou to the genius talents of Mick Minogue for his cover illustration and to Reuben Whitehouse at Rocketfuelled without whom the book wouldn't have looked half as good. Mark and Ruth Oliver for the endless cups of coffee and for keeping me fed. All the wonderful girls at Love Coffi, namely Kate Elliot, Aimee and Lily Walsh, who served coffee during the day, and fought the denizens of Hades during the night and on their days off. They are the real life Vengeance Angels!

My gratitude to those friends who provided support, criticism and kept me sane... Caroline Baldwin, Sue Baldwin and the sadly departed and much missed Les Baldwin. Abbi Gordon, Andrea and Andrew Gordon. Michael Knight and Liam Meyrick for their views on the original draft. Abigail Johnson, Jessica Hughes, Jen Baker, Paul Harrison, Eleri Jones, Lauren Holloway, Laura Welsh, Peter Spinner, Emmanuel Idowu. And of course, Jon Morris who has proved himself to be a great friend and confidant.

Finally to my family, who haven't much choice in the matter they're just stuck with me. My brother Paul Bowen, Gemma and Lewis Bowen, Jackie Greenley, Garry Williams. And the Griffiths'...Brian, Molly, Andrew and Janine.

HELL ON EARTH

A Pretty Confusing Prologue

Think of the world as an orange, a predominantly blue orange, but an orange nonetheless. Perhaps the first notable thing you will observe is that it is round. The world is round, a largely adhered to fact, or theory, depending on your point of view. It should be mentioned that a minority still believe the world is flat, like a pancake, a predominantly blue pancake, but a pancake nonetheless. This minority group are mostly members of the Flat Earth Society. This is a very small society. Even smaller as they fail to recognise the Australian contingent, simply because in a flat world they don't exist. Luckily, the Flat Earth Society still believes that a predominantly blue orange is round and therefore this simile still holds some semblance of truth for them to follow.

Now if you were to cut this orange in half, you could measure its diameter. This represents the furthest physical distance that any two points on this orange can be from each other taking a direct route. It is approximately 3.47 inches apart. Now for the world this is approximately 6,250 miles. Of course, it is impossible, or at least very difficult to pass directly through the world, so travelling around the circumference is more commonly used. For a predominantly blue orange, the distance between these two points using this method is 5.62 inches. For the world it is approximately 12,500 miles. So the furthest physical distance you can be from any object or person (including your ex) is 6,250 miles, which quite frankly is quite often not far enough. Luckily, the practical distance due to travelling restraints is 12,500 miles, which is a bit better. Unfortunately for Reg, the driver of a big, blue Volvo estate was only two blocks away.

Chapter One

It was an unusually wet day. Anyone familiar with the British climate would question this statement, as the words unusual and wet, rarely combine to describe the weather on an island which spends eighty percent of its time hiding under a rain cloud. But it was an unusually wet day. It was unusual as it wasn't raining, it hadn't rained, and showed little sign of raining. The wet part of the statement was provided by a burst water main across the street from the red bricked factory of J.P Reynolds and Son.

J.P Reynolds and Son were, as their sign informed any passers-by, manufacturers of high quality reproduction furniture. J.P Reynolds also has a daughter, but she doesn't get a mention on the sign. This wasn't due to some deep rooted misogynistic viewpoint; Porchia Reynolds had long since proved her worth to the business. Nor was it to appease some aesthetically pleasing notion. Or even because it just didn't sound right. The reason was purely economic; the signwriter at the time had charged by the letter.

J.P Reynolds' father had established the firm in 1927 under the name R.Reynolds and Son. The company had courageously survived numerous economic depressions since it was founded. The Reynolds family were fighters. During the eighties, when many of their competitors had folded, the Reynolds survived by moving to a side line of less high quality flat packed furniture. And by sacking sixty percent of their employees, sending them into destitution and enabling the Reynolds to keep the company afloat and sustain their own luxurious lifestyles. The Reynolds were fighters all right. In the last five years however, the Reynolds' firm had faced a serious downturn, they were on the verge of bankruptcy. This was largely due to one man: Reg Hallsworth. Five years ago, J.P Reynolds and Son had quite unwittingly employed a trade unionist. R.Reynolds would have turned in his grave, if he hadn't been cremated.

Reg's speeches were always greeted with the disgruntled comment 'Reg is on his soapbox again.' It wasn't really a soapbox, it was a footstool. Soapboxes are really hard to get hold of these days, cardboard packaging has taken over from the more expensive wooden boxes. Reg needed to stand on his pseudo soapbox so everyone could see him. He was not a tall man, but what he lacked in height he had gained in weight; middle age spread was starting to take control. Reg did his best to disguise his newly expanding waist line by puffing out his shirt at his belted waist, a tip he'd procured from a low budget makeover programme. His striped red necktie however, undermined this subterfuge by standing out at a forty degree angle to his body. If it hadn't been for his long light brown jacket (a garment traditionally worn by old men in hardware stores) you would have thought he was management, but Reg was definitely not management.

Reg believed in workers' rights - the right for a decent wage for a decent day's work; the right for acceptable standards of health and safety; and in the case of this protest, the right '...for quilted toilet paper, instead of the rough chafing paper that this bourgeoisie management supplies.' Most of the congregated working mass standing at the gates of the factory didn't know what Reg meant by "bourgeoisie," but it sounded good, and it meant that the "proletariat" (that was them apparently) could get another couple of days off work.

Deep down, Reg realised that his fellow workers

didn't always fully agree with his complaints against the management, and that his traditional call of "everybody out" always seemed to receive a greater response on sunny days and friday afternoons. This time however, he knew he had the full backing of his comrades, chafing toilet paper affected everyone. The proof of this was the turn out he had received for his protest, it wasn't particularly sunny or a friday and the workforce was out in strength. The fact that the local team was in the quarter finals and kick off was at one thirty completely by-passed Reg. He was in his element. He saw himself as King in his dream speech, Mao waving his little red book, or Lenin spurring on the honest workers into revolution. He had the attention of his working comrades, and his cause was just.

'No longer shall we suffer the indignity of rough toilet tissue, comrades we stand united.'

As Reg's tirade against the "bloodsucking management" continued, the "honest hard working men" began to become restless, shuffling their feet, shifting their weight as impatience rose amongst them. All they wanted to hear was the call for strike action. They could say *aye* in favour, go home, put their team's paraphernalia on and get down the pub to watch the game on the big screen. Such events required a reasonable level of drunken stupor prior to the game's commencement, and time was ticking. The driver of the big blue Volvo estate was now only one block away: His name was Norris.

09.32 a.m. Norris was asleep. He knew he was asleep because he wasn't panicking about being late. The alarm clock rang. He hit the snooze button and was asleep again. He always set the alarm early so he could get an *extra* five minutes in bed. The next two times he hit the snooze button, he didn't bother to wake up. The next time the alarm rang Norris was awake. He knew he was awake because he was panicking about being late. With all the practise he'd had, the casual observer may have thought he'd be quite good at waking up, he wasn't. Shit! thought Norris. He was late. Norris never swore out loud but he did possess an extensive vocabulary of swear words which he often thought of during times of necessity, such as being late for a not particularly important business meeting. Nothing in Norris' life was particularly important. Unfortunately, he didn't know this. Shit was one of his favourite expletives, he thought it again, shit! He was late for his meeting with the assistant to the assistant under-manager's section assistant of region 105. You don't get higher than that thought Norris.

Twenty nine minutes and seven seconds later Norris reversed his big blue Volvo estate out of his driveway, and sped off down the pleasant suburban street where he lived alone, without any cats. If he was lucky, traffic wouldn't be too bad and he'd still make the meeting in plenty of time. As he reached the end of the street, Norris remembered he wasn't lucky. He joined the back of an exceptionally long queue of cars, commonly referred to as a traffic jam. Norris was an old hand at being stuck in traffic jams and quickly resorted to his familiar regime of moving slowly behind the car in front. Years of practice had honed his skills in this department. As he crawled down the street he divided his attention between watching the back of the car in front, the digital clock slowly ticking vital minutes away and pedestrians rapidly overtaking him on the inside. Every so often the whirring clatter of a cyclist weaving between the immobile cars broke his thoughts. Although not a very vindictive man, as he watched the cyclists whizzing past, dangerously close to his car's wing mirrors, Norris wished for heavy rain. It didn't really matter though, because as soon as the traffic started moving he'd overtake each and every one of them, but for now rain would be good.

As his dashboard clock ticked another vital minute away Norris' leg began to twitch, in an outward sign of his internal turmoil and panic. 10.19 didn't seem half as bad as 10.20. Norris began to list alternative routes in his head, two of which quickly rose to the top as the most viable to get him to the meeting on time. The choices were, heading right down Bedford Street and hoping the traffic lights were with him, or taking the less direct route past the factory J.P Reynolds and Son, where the roads should be less congested enabling him to travel faster.

Whilst Norris contemplated these two choices he was unaware, as is often the case, that he was not in fact only making the choice of which route was quicker. He was also making a life changing *if only* decision. The kind of decision that often passes unnoticed, until, with a sudden blast of hindsight, the protagonist realises where it all went wrong, and proclaims *if only I'd...* Norris chose the latter route. At this point he truly believed he had made the right decision, the road was almost completely clear, of course he didn't realise which decision he had actually made.

Norris pressed heavily on the accelerator and his car responded, he leant across to the radio and switched it on. He looked back up. To his great surprise a number of workmen had decided to undertake work on a burst water main in the middle of the road. He pulled hard on the steering wheel, avoiding the workmen and heading towards the entrance of J.P Reynolds and Son. Where, to his further surprise, a large group of workers were congregated outside. With the speed, agility and almost catlike instincts of a puma, Norris took both his hands off the wheel and screamed.

09.32. Death had had a lie in. It'd been a late night, playing poker with the boys. The boys, in this case, were the Four Horsemen of Everyday Life, lower profile than their Apocalypse counterparts, but still very important in the regulation of the human population. They were Casual Violence, (a lot more sensitive than his name implied and generally quite a nice guy) Suicide, (the joker of the pack, he always had a good story to tell about work) Negligence, (the Romeo of the group and also the outright winner of last night's game, he cheated both with women and cards) and Accidental Misadventure (his friends generally referred to him by his nickname; Oops. He was in charge of accidents and always brought his work home with him. To be honest, Death found him to be quite boring, but he was all right when he wasn't complaining). Negligence and Oops had both been quite busy lately due to the increased popularity of home improvement and DIY, a field in which their work often overlapped. Both had felt the need to blow off some steam, so what had started out as a few quiet drinks soon turned into a mammoth session. It had been a rough night, too much to drink, too much money lost, and a busy day ahead, but life was like that for Death.

Death isn't the only Death. With the ever expanding population it's far too much work for one person. Death as an occupation has always been a popular field for *souls* to enter. With excellent job security, a good medical and dental plan, and a reasonable pension on top, there is always a good response from hopeful applicants. Unsurprisingly, Death as a profession is highly popular with the type that would have chosen accountancy on Earth. Few applicants however, have the flair and imagination that a really good

Death requires. The Death in this case, and dubiously entitled hero, is in fact Death Third Class, Number 221, of the Human Transition Department. The Human Transition Department deals with the relocation of souls to their ordained destination.

Death looked in the mirror and poked his tongue out. Not too bad, he thought. He needed a shave but he could get away with it. He checked his schedule as he put on his pinstriped suit and wide collared bright purple shirt, no tie. Death had a groovy disco style dress sense. He'd been a high flier in the department until a decade or so ago. The youngest Death to become Third Class, the future had looked pretty rosy. Department heads predicted his rise to Head of Natural Disasters within a millennium, but then it all went wrong. He accidentally relocated Father Tobias to Hell, a fairly small mistake easily rectified granted, but unfortunately for Death Father Tobias happened to be a very close friend of God. There was uproar, promotion opportunities evaporated, and to make matters worse his long term girlfriend left him when the scandal broke out. He began to question his existence. There didn't appear to be a future in death anymore.

Death tore himself away from the mirror. He looked good, in spite of the previous night. He picked up a pile of papers that were innocently lying on his side table, stuffed them into his briefcase and left the house. As he closed the door behind him, a single piece of paper fell from the unlocked briefcase and blew away on a passing breeze. As the piece of paper floated happily away it had little idea of the trouble it was going to cause, because it was a piece of paper. If it had known, it still wouldn't have cared because it was after all, a piece of paper.

When faced with a large blue Volvo estate careering towards them, most members of the animal kingdom, including man, will take evasive action. This is not the case with the hedgehog. The hedgehog will rely on its evolutionary tactic of rolling into a ball and bracing itself for impact. This is one of the reasons why man is considered superior to the hedgehog.

To many, man is considered to be evolutionarily superior to all members of the animal kingdom. Science would have us believe that this is due to greater intelligence and opposable thumbs. This is not entirely true. No matter how you look at it, in evolutionary terms and the game of survival, mankind basically cheated. We did not develop an unrivalled speed and agility, an infallible defence; involving prickly spikes or an armoured shell, or even pretty big teeth. We didn't adapt our form at all. We just picked up something and hit our rivals in the food chain with it. In the sporting world we would have been disqualified for the use of unfair equipment. We even cheated in the evolution of the hunt. Whilst other species evolved to increase their effectiveness, we locked our intended prey in a field, waited till they got fat, then ate them.

As the Volvo sped towards Reg, he completely ignored the evolutionary trait of evasion. Instead he opted for the hedgehog's technique; he crouched down and braced for impact. Whether due to some inherent evolutionary flaw or just plain panic, it's hard to say, however, the result was much the same as the hedgehog's.

Reg stood over his body. Nearby, a Volvo estate was parked, with the expertise that only a drunk can manage, but the driver wasn't drunk, he'd just been in an accident. Something isn't quite right thought Reg as he looked down at his body, then it occurred to him. He'd been in an accident. He'd been in an accident with a big blue Volvo estate.

Reg had read an article once about an out of body experience, that must be what's happening, he mused. He was incredibly calm considering recent events. Quite a crowd was gathering around his comatose body, like a squawking flock of seagulls around a discarded pasty, wings flapping as they jostled for a better position. Reg remembered the person in the article had seen a bright white light and when... Tom, that was his name, had turned his back on it he'd found himself back in his body. Reg looked around for a bright white light, he couldn't see a bright white light, there was no bright white light, he began to panic. If there was no bright white light how could he get back into his body. He tried to climb back into his body, but that wasn't working.

'Help!' yelled Reg.

No-one listened.

'Help!' he yelled a bit louder.

Still no-one listened. His pleas for help were interrupted by a woman pushing through the crowd.

'I'm a doctor,' said the woman in a business like fashion.

It reminded Reg of that riddle he'd once heard.

'Now this is more like it!' said Reg, as the woman knelt down next to his body and began C.P.R. Reg didn't know what it stood for but he was quite sure that was what she was doing.

Peters from the shop floor came across to help her. Reg had campaigned to get a qualified first-aider working every shift. He'd been right to call a strike action over it and now everyone could see he'd been right. The management couldn't argue cost effectiveness now. One-nil to the proletariat. He gazed up towards the management windows and stuck two fingers up, after all, they couldn't see him. His attention flitted back to his comatose body. The woman was rising from her knees and putting her hand on Peters' shoulder.

'We can't do any more,' she said softly.

'What do you mean, you can't do any more!' yelled Reg, but she wasn't listening.

'Too bad,' replied Peters nonchalantly.

'Too bad, too bad! What do you mean too bad? I'm a shining light, a beacon of hope to you people, and that's all you've got to say!' The panic came through in Reg's voice. 'Come on comrades, I'm dying here!'

Interestingly, when most people exclaim "I'm dying here," they're just expressing a sincere need for help. Unfortunately for Reg however, on this occasion, the expression was no mere exaggerated plea, it was the truth. Although he wasn't using the correct tense. Reg was not dying; Reg was dead.

Reg slumped his out of body experience down on the kerb.

'I'm dead,' he said to no-one in particular, but no-one in particular listened. Looking down at his dead body, he noticed a bald patch on the back of his head for the first time, which he found quite unsettling. It's funny how life's vanity stays with you after you die.

'I'm dead,' he repeated.

'Certainly looks that way,' replied no-one in particular from behind him.

Reg had already become quite accustomed to no-one replying, so it came as quite a shock.

'I'm dead,' he repeated again, just in case he was going insane and hearing voices, as well as being dead. I mean how bad can a day get.

'That's right.'

Reg turned around. Looking down at him stood a tall man, a lot taller than Reg, at least six foot five inches although it was difficult to tell from his sitting position. He wore a dark single-breasted pin stripe suit, with a wide collared bright purple shirt, and had a smile as wide as his collars. Several thoughts shot through Reg's mind at once, perhaps the most significant being, that this guy looked cool and was definitely going to try and sell him something. Death opened his briefcase and took out a sheet of paper.

'Reg...' he enquired.

'Yes.' Now Reg knew he was going to sell him something. Perhaps life assurance, that would be quite handy given the circumstances.

'Sorry I'm late. I'm Death Third Class, Number 221 of the Human Transition Department.'

'You're who?'

'Death Third Class, Number 221 of the...'

'Yeah, I got that. Death? The Death?'

'Yep Death.' Death put on a deep spooky voice. 'The Grim Reaper, Ferryman for the River Stix. Of course, there's more than one of us, far too much work for one, it's a big department. But I'm your Death.'

'Oh.'

Death's smile began to fade. 'What?'

'It's just... I just thought.'

'What?' Death asked.

'It's just I thought you know...'

Death did know but let Reg continue anyway.

'...you'd look more like Death.'

'Ah huh.'

Reg thought this meant I don't quite understand please explain. It didn't, it meant oh well here we go again.

'I thought you'd have a black cloak, be carrying a scythe... that sort of thing...'

Death's mind wandered off as Reg rambled on about what he should be wearing. People were always commenting on the whole black cloak look. That image was so fourteenth century. Granted it was a good look and inspired fear and awe, but fashions change. Anyway, the modern guidelines of the Human Transition Department dictated that attire should present a *friendlier and more welcoming look.*

'Hey, hey, come back!' shouted Reg.

His yell broke into Death's thoughts. Death gave a slow leaden sigh as he watched Reg pursue the ambulance down the street. Three blocks later, a gasping Reg gave up the chase.

'Please bring back my body, I haven't finished with it yet,' he whined.

Death appeared next to Reg and put his hand on his shoulder. Reg thought this meant your time's up, you're coming with me. It didn't, it meant I'm really sorry this had to happen to you, you seem like a nice bloke and you have my sympathy. It was all part of the new friendlier approach of the Human Transition Department. Reg should be forgiven for his mistake. When Death puts his hand on your shoulder, its easy to think the worst.

'Never mind Reg, you're going to a much better place...' Death paused in his sympathetic speech. 'I think.'

Whilst Death rummaged through his briefcase, checking to see if he was in fact going to a better place, Reg felt like he was going to have a heart attack. Fortunately for Reg, he was already dead, so there was little chance of him suffering any form of coronary seizure, but then again sometimes even a cloud's silver lining doesn't stop it from being a dreary day. Death quickly scanned his eyes over a newly produced form.

'Yep definitely a better place,' confirmed Death.

In spite of recent events this cheered Reg up.

Death clicked his fingers, and an elevator appeared out of thin air. People often have some difficulty trying to conceptualise what something appearing out of thin air is actually like. Now if you were to stand in a dark room and turn the light on, you would suddenly be able to see any objects in that room. This is not comparable to something appearing out of thin air. If you were to witness the actual light appear in the room, this would be a much better comparison. Needless to say, Reg gave a slight jolt of shock as the elevator appeared. Death made a polite indication to move towards it, as if inviting him to dine at a rather expensive restaurant. Perhaps Reg would have made small talk and commented on the plush interior of the lift, with its deep red cushioned walls and gold trim and hand rails, but small talk was not on his agenda. His attention was largely fixed on the lift's control panel. It had two buttons; arrows indicated up and down. A tinny instrumental version of a popular song began as Death pressed the up button. Reg couldn't quite place the song, he definitely knew it though. The tinny tune slowly seeped into his consciousness and fixed itself firmly in a place where it could appear periodically to irritate its host. The irritating little tune finally got the better of Reg, and he decided to ask Death what it was. Death was not the usual person you would ask about pop trivia, but as the lift had no other occupants, Reg had no choice.

'I've gotta ask...' began Reg.

'I know what you're going to say,' interrupted Death, although his next sentence proved that he didn't. 'You thought that there would be a stairway leading up to Heaven.'

Reg would have corrected Death on this point, but now come to think of it, he was intrigued as to why there wasn't a stairway.

'Well,' continued Death. 'The stairway was so time consuming The Department decided to move with the times, and install an elevator.'

In fact, although the stairway was indeed more time consuming than the elevator, neither are actually necessary. Both Heaven and Hell require no actual physical travelling at all. They both exist on separate planes of existence, and *souls*, as dead people are commonly referred to in the afterlife, can instantly pass from one plane to another. However, souls generally had a problem with this concept, so after an in-depth survey, in which eighty-seven percent of souls found difficulty with pan-dimensional plane theory, it was deemed that some act of travelling to the destination would ease the soul's sense of transition.

The lift stopped and the doors opened with a *ping*. The *ping* was also a recent addition, it apparently helped souls understand that their *travelling* time was over.

Chapter two

Norris sat in the back of a police car. As is often the case when sitting in a police car, he was not happy. As standard procedure he had been given a breath test, he'd passed with flying colours. The police officer had asked if he had smoked a cigarette in the last ten minutes, it apparently affected the result, he hadn't smoked a cigarette in six years. He wanted a cigarette. Norris sat there waiting for the officer to return, he'd been quite nice and understanding, but Norris knew how this sort of thing worked. Any minute another police officer would turn up and hit him across the head several times with his truncheon. Good cop, bad cop it was the oldest trick in the book.

The good cop returned.

'We're just locking up your car,' he informed Norris 'You'll have to accompany us to the station I'm afraid. The accident has proved fatal.'

Norris' world came crashing in around him. He'd killed someone. He'd be sent to prison. He'd probably left some woman a widow, with small children asking *when is daddy coming home?* He'd never make the meeting on time. Where did that thought come from? How could he think about the meeting now? The guilt Norris felt for thinking that thought added to the already huge black mass of remorse he was feeling. He was a nice guy, nice guys didn't think of themselves at times like these, maybe he wasn't a nice guy. Still, he did feel guilty about having that thought, so maybe he was a nice guy after all. Besides, just because things were going wrong in his life, didn't mean he should let others down. It was only right that he should think of his prior commitments. Really he should give them a call, just to let them know he would not make the meeting, it was the right thing to do. He made the call.

'Hello, it's Norris, I won't be able to make the meeting, I've been in an accident. Yeah, I know it's a real pain.'

Norris slowly glanced up to see the faces of two disapproving police officers. From their looks he realised they didn't think he was a nice guy. Now it wasn't a case of good cop, bad cop, it was bad cop, bad cop.

Two hours later, Norris left the Police Station. It had been a surreal experience, not in the literal sense: the walls didn't change colour and go wavy and no cows flew past. It had been surreal in the *that doesn't often happen to me* way. Norris was not the kind of person that frequented police stations. Naturally he had been to one before, the time he'd reported his lawnmower stolen for one, but never on the possibly wrong side of the law way. It didn't start too well. The only lawyers that Norris knew about were injury claim specialists, and apparently they didn't really deal with his sort of case. Although, should his fears of suffering police brutality whilst in the cells prove true, they were sure they could get him compensation. The desk sergeant finally helped him get a lawyer, after muttering something along the lines of 'I haven't got time for this idiot to keep messing me around.' But perhaps the most embarrassing moment came during the interview, when Norris, feeling the pressure, yelled he was innocent at the people behind the two way mirror, which turned out to be an ordinary mirror. The interviewing police officer had finally assured Norris that he was unlikely to be sent to prison for the day's events, in light of the fact that the road works had not been properly sign posted and the negligence lay with them.

Furthermore, he didn't feel the need for prosecuting Norris over the ice lolly he'd stolen when he was ten. Norris was free to go. He was even offered a lift home by the two police officers who had brought him in, but Norris eyed their truncheons and declined. He didn't want to suffer at the hands of a bad cop, bad cop routine, in spite of assurances of compensation from Lawyers R Us.

As he walked out of the front door of the Police Station he felt like Nelson Mandela finally leaving enforced captivity. He took an exaggerated deep breath of that sweet, sweet, fresh air and mumbled the words 'free at last, free at last, praise the Lord, I'm free at last.' Of course, it was Martin Luther King who spoke those immortal words not Nelson Mandela, but Norris didn't know that.

Norris watched as cyclists and pedestrians overtook him on his drive back home. It wasn't the traffic that slowed him down this time, it was his conscience. Eventually he pulled into his driveway. Stepping out of his car he gave a cursory wave to the sullen guy at number twelve as he walked his dog past Norris' house. No response. He must know thought Norris. Soon everyone would know. He was a murderer. Norris entered his house and made his way to the fridge, pulling out a carton of milk. He took two long gulps. He never drank out of the carton, it was the start of things to come. He pulled his tie off, it got stuck halfway over his head. After a second's struggle he left it there, like some jungle dwelling freedom fighter from an eighties' film. He stripped the rest of his clothes off and stood naked in his kitchen. This is great he thought. This is freedom.

Then it happened. For the first time ever he began to truly think about his life. The day's events made him realise that life could be short. Just like the guy he killed, it could end just like that. Death could turn up in his black cloak, carrying a scythe and take you away. He began to think about what he'd actually done with his life, and when you've had a life like Norris' this is a dangerous line of thought to take. Robert Frost once wrote that he took *the path less travelled* in his life and that *made all the difference.* Norris took the more commonly used, well sign posted path, that didn't go further than the local shops.

'That's it,' said Norris aloud. 'I am going to change my life, and not just some of the things, but everything!'

To Norris this was a life changing liberation, an insightful revelation... It was his epiphany! To everyone else it was a nervous breakdown.

Norris' first life changing decision involved work. He didn't want to be a sales representative for the leading manufacturer of office stationery anymore. He wanted to discover sunken treasure for a living. The first step was easy; quit work. So he made a phone call.

'Hello this is Norris, I don't want to work for you anymore. I'm going to discover Blackbeard's treasure instead.'

That had been easy.

The next stage was a bit more complex. Even for his new found self, Norris realised there were certain restrictions to following his new career. The first to overcome, was the fact that he couldn't actually scuba dive, and from what he understood about finding sunken treasure, it required a certain amount of underwater work. But his ever optimistic new self argued that he had snorkelled before and that was the same thing really. Nevertheless, he decided to book a couple of lessons, before heading out to the wide blue yonder. So with another quick phone call, he enrolled in the local diving school's intensive six week course, which included a complimentary tee-shirt.

The next step was to build a tree house in the back garden. To the rational mind tree house building does little to aid a career in sunken treasure hunting, but it made perfect sense to Norris. Putting on his dressing gown, and taking his credit cards from the side table (even treasure hunters needed to pay for things) Norris headed to the local hardware store to purchase the materials needed for his tree house. One hour later, he returned with the equipment he needed to undertake his task.

Now you may have expected Norris to have had some difficulty acquiring his materials dressed as he was, or at least to have received a funny look or two from the employees at the store. As it happened, they were extremely helpful, and even aided him in buying items he didn't even need. Apparently, this sort of thing is a common occurrence, as hardware stores are often frequented by people with less than rational minds.

With no discernible woodworking skill, Norris found little trouble in doing a botch job of building his tree house. As he sat back and admired his work, he decided he would live in his tree house from now on. This type of behaviour would have certainly roused the suspicion of the neighbours if it hadn't been for the fact that he lived in a quite suburban street, where the best way to confront the strange behaviour of a neighbour was to ignore it and hope they'd move soon. Not that his behaviour wasn't noticed, it was, but the twitching of net curtains was quickly followed with the sentiment *best not get involved*. Had Ed Gein, one of America's most infamous serial killers, decided to live there he'd probably still be continuing his grizzly work today. In fact, there was the distinct possibility that a gruesome serial killer did live in the vicinity of Norris' house. The sullen guy at number twelve was always digging in his back garden late at night, but well *best not get involved*. So Norris, with the aid of his apathetic neighbours, was able to freely continue with his epiphany undisturbed. However, there was someone who was concerned with Norris' behaviour. Her name was Jenny.

Jenny was an Angel, not in the sense of she's a really nice, caring person, although she was. Jenny was an Angel in the celestial body kind of way. Jenny was Norris' Angel, not in the sense of *she's a girl I'm kind of going out with*, but in the Guardian Angel type of way.

The Guardian Angels are the most overworked Angels in Heaven, often having to take on the guardianship of several hundred people at once. Their workload is commonly aided by volunteers. These volunteers or Guardian Souls as they are affectionately referred to, most often consist of deceased relatives willing to give up some of their free time to support their loved ones on Earth. None of Norris' deceased relatives "really had the time" to undertake this role, and so Jenny took on his guardianship. Unfortunately, Jenny was not the best at her job, some of the other Guardian Angels felt she was too self absorbed, but this was far from the truth, she really did care for people. Jenny's problem was, (for want of a sacrilegious word) she was a bit dippy. Not for want of trying, her success rates were poor. She just kind of got things wrong every now and then. Like the time when she had been assigned to convincing a young man not to kill himself, a few gentle words and he had been motivated to live on and follow his dream. How was she supposed to know that there were in fact two Adolf Hitlers living in that part of Bavaria at that moment time, both wanting to kill themselves, I mean what are the odds of that!

'I don't know if I'm really cut out for this job,'

said Jenny, over a steaming cup of hot chocolate.

Her friend, Angel Lucy, took a sip of her decaf latte, and looked up with sympathetic eyes.

'Course you are Jen. You're a really good Angel.'

'It's like that time with Adolf Hitler...'

'You're not still going on about that? It wasn't your fault, it could have happened to anyone.' Lucy wasn't really sure it could have happened to anyone but she knew Jenny was still sensitive over the matter.

'It wouldn't have happened to Judith,' said Jenny, in a sulky retort.

'Yeah, well Judith's got glitter coming out of her bottom,' replied Lucy.

Angels are not particularly good at insulting people, so Jenny and Lucy should be forgiven for the rupture of laughter that this statement caused. Jenny wiped the laughter tears from her eyes and looked earnestly at Lucy.

'I'm going to get this one right, it's a guy called Norris, he really needs help,' Jenny proclaimed, firm-jawed.

'That's the spirit Jen, you go girl.'

Norris slept soundly in his tree house, his body bathed in bright moonlight, but it wasn't moonlight that protected him through his slumber from the guy at number twelve, it was the protective wings of his Guardian Angel Jenny.

Norris woke late the following morning, to a commotion a few doors down at number twelve.

'Psst. psst. Can you see what's happening from up there?' It was his next door neighbour, George.

George had married the woman of his dreams six years ago. He often wondered where she was now. His wife stood next to him craning her neck over the fence facing number twelve. George was a middle aged man in his late twenties, his wife had nagged his life expectancy down to around the mid-forties range. From his tree house Norris could clearly see the back garden of number twelve.

'The police are there, they seem to be digging up the patio,' said Norris, relaying the information he saw.

'Then it's true. I knew it!' exclaimed George clicking his fingers.

'What's true?' asked Norris, as he jumped down from his tree house.

'Well, I've always thought he was a bit strange, that guy at number twelve, digging the garden in the middle of the night, that sort of thing.'

It was okay to admit to noticing the strange behaviour of your neighbours, after the authorities were involved.

'Apparently, last night, he wandered into the Police Station, claiming to be a mass murderer, the victims all buried in his back garden.'

'Wow.'

'It gets better,' continued George. 'He said he was on his way to kill his next victim, when, get this, an Angel, you know with feathery wings and such, blocked his path and convinced him to confess. I mean how crazy can you get. No offence meant.'

'None taken,' replied Norris as he wasn't quite sure why he should take offence.

'Okay, this is the really creepy thing.' George was getting really excited with the story now. 'Do you know how he picked out his victims?'

Norris shrugged, in a negative response.

'He'd walk his dog and anyone who spoke to him, waved or even smiled...' George gestured a slicing motion across his neck '...schlick.'

'I'd better get going,' said Norris, his heart pounding.

'Well I for one, am going to take more notice of my neighbours' behaviour from now on,' said George casually, as Norris walked back into his house, completely naked apart from the blue paint he covered himself with the night before. 'You just don't know what types are out there.'

If Norris had any deeply buried doubts over his recent actions, they vanished like a pay packet on a Saturday night. He knew his life had been meaningless and he'd had a sign. His life could have ended last night and what did he have to show for it, well apart from a great tree house, nothing. More drastic action was required, but first he'd wash this stupid blue paint off. It was supposed to be green, it'd looked green in the moonlight last night.

Jenny was back in the coffee shop, with Lucy. Last night's events had not gone according to plan, so she'd called an emergency crisis meeting.

'I was supposed to help him and now he's worse,' sobbed Jenny.

'Come on Jen, you saved his life!' Lucy put her hand on Jenny's shoulder to emphasis her words of support.

'He's having a crisis, he might do something stupid.'

'What like painting himself blue?'

Jenny gave a sniffled laugh at this, Lucy always cheered her up.

'You know what I mean, something dangerous.'

Lucy sipped her decaf latte, deep in thought for a moment.

'Why don't I take on your other guardianships for a bit. So you can concentrate on Norris. Maybe try a hands on approach?'

Jenny looked up hopefully. 'Can you manage the extra workload?'

'Of course I can babe, you just concentrate on Norris.'

'A hands on approach would be good. But well, what should I wear?'

'Leave that to me. If there's one thing I know, it's how to shop.'

The two Angels left arm in arm and headed towards Joan of Arc Boulevard, where all the best designer shops were situated.

Norris stood at the pool edge, looking at his fellow classmates in the local diving school's six week intensive course. They were seven in total, a mixture of men and women, all studying each other while waiting for Pete, their diving instructor. The first ones that caught Norris' eye were two young women; Sue and Helen. They had obviously come together, both were quite attractive and both were looking at Glen. Glen was a tall, well toned, and artificially tanned man, who'd instantly introduced himself with a corny but well received joke and a confirmation that he was the alpha male of this group. Norris was vying for second place in the manly stakes with Simon. He was obviously a computer geek, but he was doing this for charity and could win on the nice guy ticket. Luckily, Norris had dropped in the fact that he was pursuing a career in sunken treasure hunting, that was sure to impress. The other guy in the group, Tony, didn't enter the equation. He was learning to dive for his honeymoon and was quite frankly a bit ugly, added to which, he was with his equally unattractive fiancé, Liz. Besides it didn't look like Tony or Liz were going to interact much with the group. So far they'd spent the whole time glued to each other whispering private jokes back and forth. Norris had the distinct feeling his skimpy trunks had been the topic of one such joke. Pete, the course instructor, came out of his office at the side of the pool. He was slightly overweight and slightly over-tanned, his hairy chest was turning grey and he spoke in a voice far too loud for the acoustics of the indoor pool.

'Okay class, I need you to partner up, come on into twos.' He emphasised the need for haste with a couple of loud claps.

Norris instantly panicked, it was like picking teams at school again. Please don't let me be last. Tony and Liz were already together. Glen quickly moved in on Helen, the slightly more attractive of the two remaining women. Helen gave a little apologetic shrug towards a disgruntled Sue, as she partnered up with Glen. This was it, Norris and Simon both looked at each other, then at Sue, but before they could move, Sue walked over to Simon. She couldn't have heard Norris say about his career in sunken treasure hunting.

'Where's your partner?' Pete asked Norris in an accusing manner.

This was a perfect opportunity for Norris to show he was a strong individual, more intelligent and witty than this uneducated oaf of a diving instructor. A sarcastic line about two not dividing into seven should do it.

'Er.. not sure, haven't got one. Sorry.'

'There's supposed to be eight of you.' Pete still directed his complaint towards Norris.

'Sorry, but, er, I came alone,' apologised Norris, although he was not sure why.

'Very well, you'll have to double up.'

Not Tony and Liz, not Tony and Liz, not Tony and Liz.

'Join them,' said Pete, pointing to Tony and Liz.

Tony and Liz's faces indicated that they were even more unhappy than Norris with this forced arrangement.

And then she walked in. She was, without a doubt, the most beautiful woman Norris had ever seen. More beautiful than any film actress or model, more beautiful than the woman at the local chip shop before she opened her mouth. She had long blonde hair and blue eyes. Not just blue eyes but really blue eyes, stunning blue eyes, wow amazing blue eyes. Then Norris looked down at her bikini wrapped body. Gulp. He quickly looked up. She was looking at him with those eyes. The other men in the group had seen her too. Glen was pushing out his chest and squinting his eyes in a way that he thought made him look like a young Clint Eastwood. Tony had released Liz from his clutches for the first time since they had arrived, and Simon had actually begun to shake. Norris had little doubt in his mind, she was an angel sent down from heaven. Not in a literal sense of course, that would be crazy.

'Hi, I'm Jenny, sorry I'm late everybody. Oh good, are we getting into groups?'

Jenny walked straight over to Norris, despite Glen's attempts to snare her on her way past, by pushing Helen towards Norris. Jenny immediately put her hand in Norris' hand and whispered.

'This is going to be fun, don't you think?'

Norris was too busy trying to faint to reply, but Jenny just squeezed his hand tighter, her shoulders raising slightly as she gave a little giggle.

'I've just got to go to my office, a minute,' said Pete, adjusting the front of his trunks as he left.

'I'm Jenny, if you missed it,' said Jenny softly into Norris' ear.

How could she think I could have missed her name? It's already painted on my heart. He wanted to tell her this, but he settled for a slightly less romantic, British version.

'I'm Norris, pleased to meet you.'

He went to shake hands with her but realised she already held his hand, so he raised it slightly and gave it a little wobble. Jenny laughed at this, in a decidedly non mocking way. She genuinely liked Norris, he was funny and quite cute. Maybe it wouldn't be such a chore being his guardian.

'So what do you do for a living?' Jenny asked,

as she looked deep into his eyes.

For some reason, Norris didn't want to brag that he was a sunken treasure hunter, even though he was. He looked deeper into her eyes. For some reason he wanted to tell her that he was just an ordinary guy, a sales representative something like that. He wanted her to like him for who he was, not for what he did or how great his life was. But that was who he was, Norris the sunken treasure hunter. Why didn't he want her to know about his life changing liberation, his epiphany? It didn't make sense, but for some reason Norris wanted to be plain old Norris again. A voice broke Norris' thoughts.

'Sorry, 'bout that class. Lets all get into the water,' resounded Pete's booming voice.

Norris the sunken treasure hunter entered the water.

Later that night Norris couldn't quite remember why living in a tree house was so important to being a sunken treasure hunter, he also forgot to paint himself green. He decided to sleep in his own bed and he dreamt of Jenny.

Jenny sat in the coffee shop waiting for Lucy to arrive.

'A small decaf latte, please,' Lucy shouted to the barrista, as she entered.

'Hi, Luce.'

'Sorry I'm late babe. I've had a terrible day. That idiot, Jonny *the human cannonball* Jones, decided he was going to be shot through two hoops of fire. If I hadn't created a downpour, he would've been toast. How did you get on with Norris?'

'Great, Judith couldn't have done better. I think I've made him really start to come to his senses.'

'Oh, well done you,' encouraged Lucy.

'He dreamt of me last night.'

'He what?'

'He said my name out loud in his sleep, I think he likes me.'

'Jen,' Lucy attempted to interrupt.

'He's really quite cute.'

A worried expression crept over Lucy's face.

'You're not falling for him are you?'

'Of course not.'

Lucy's voice took on the tone of a disapproving parent.

'Jenny.'

'No. He's just kind of fun to hang with, that's all. That's all!'

'Jenny,' Lucy's voice now took on a slightly more concerned tone. 'I know you, you're falling for him. You know it won't work, he's a mortal.'

'No I'm not, really. He's just fun, that's all.'

'Just be careful, okay?'

'Yes, Luce. Now tell me all about your day. What is it with Jonny Jones? Has he got a death wish or something?'

As Lucy related all the highs and lows of her day, Jenny's mind wandered. She felt guilty about not paying Lucy her full attention, but not even Angels are perfect all of the time. Jenny began to wonder if she was falling for Norris. She couldn't be, could she? Angels and mortals falling in love, it was the oldest story in the world, and it always ended in tragedy. No she thought firmly to herself, she was not going to fall in love with a mortal. Definitely not. But he did make her laugh.

'Oh, crap!' said Cupid from his nearby seat.

Chapter 3

Bacchaus sat in the penthouse suite of the most exclusive hotel in London. The luxurious interior suited the human form that he was displaying. Bacchaus was a Demon. Not just any Demon, he was a particularly evil Demon. Even amongst his fellow minions of the Underworld, he was considered 'a bad un.' Bacchaus was Satan's right hand man, Chief Whip of the Underworld. When his fellow Demons were slacking or just plain not being evil enough, it was Bacchaus that brought them into line. He was one of the few that referred to themselves as Dark Angels, Satan was the only true Dark or Fallen Angel, but he allowed Bacchaus to use this title as, well quite frankly, he was so good at his job. Bacchaus' pastimes included ethnic cleansing and genocide, plagues and famine, and badminton. Of the seven deadly sins he liked to have a hand in all of them. It had been he, The Dark Angel Bacchaus, that had tricked Angel Jenny into saving the wrong person in Bavaria, and now apparently she was back on the scene. This would be fun, in the particularly evil Demon sense of the word.

A knock at the door broke Bacchaus from his evil machinations.

'Room service,' piped a voice from the other side of the door.

'Enter!' replied Bacchaus, in a deep booming voice.(He was a Demon after all and deep booming voices and demonic characterisation sort of go hand in hand.)

The waiter wheeled in a trolley, carrying Bacchaus' breakfast. Bacchaus handed over a fifty pound tip and waved him away. He knew the waiter would spend the money feeding his cocaine habit. He always enjoyed being a patron of drug addiction.

This was a well earned breakfast, he'd had a busy few days. He rarely bothered *getting his hands dirty*, usually letting others do his dirty work, but this had been quite important. Not that it sounded important, arranging a burst water main, creating a traffic jam and instigating an eleven a.m. meeting, he'd only had to *call in* a few favours. Bacchaus took a bite of his scrambled egg. Not enough pepper! He would have vengeance for this. He concentrated on the waiter that had just served him, and muttered a guttural incantation.

Luck is a very unusual thing. Its balance is precarious; a lack of luck in one individual often leads to too much luck in another, and *visa versa*. The equilibrium must be maintained, or world wide calamity would ensue. Bacchaus was an expert in the alteration of luck. He paused for a moment, and listened to the *crash*, as the waiter fell down two flights of stairs. He waited for the *snap* of his neck, before he continued with his breakfast. Actually, come to think of it, the eggs were perfect.

'We're here,' said Death cheerfully, indicating to Reg to step out of the lift.

Reg was unsurprisingly nervous about seeing Heaven for the first time, people usually had to wait their whole lives before seeing Heaven. He slowly stepped out of the elevator.

'Oh,' said Reg, obviously very disappointed.

'What?'

'Well I just thought Heaven would be, well nice,' said Reg looking around. 'This is just... kind of grey.'

'Oh this isn't Heaven.'

A chest tightening panic struck Reg to the core, if this wasn't Heaven, then it must be, oh no! Think of an alternative, think of an alternative, Heaven and ... Heaven and...

'Heaven is over there.'

'What? This isn't Hell?'

'No, Heaven's behind that cloud bank, we gotta get you registered first,' said Death chuckling.

'I've got to register?'

'Of course,' replied Death. 'Heaven is a private members club, only good people can get in.'

Death loved that line and used it as often as he could. It wasn't really his line, he'd stolen it from a television evangelist, but as that evangelist was now doing time in Hell for embezzling hundreds of thousands of dollars from the old and vulnerable, he figured he could pass it off as his own.

'Come on Reggie boy let's get you registered. It's that grey building over there.'

Reg took a step forward and stumbled, beneath his feet was a cattle grid.

'What's that doing there?' he asked.

'That's the gate to Heaven.'

'Wait a minute, the Gate to Heaven is a cattle grid? Not the Pearly Gates, or some lavish wrought silver masterpiece?'

Death looked genuinely bewildered by Reg's expectation. 'Why would you bother having some fancy gate, when your main nemesis, the guy you most want to keep out, has cloven hooves for feet?'

Reg conceded Death certainly had a point. The whole Pearly Gate thing did seem a bit ridiculous when you thought of it that way.

The offices for the Registration of Souls looked like every other office block Reg had ever been to. He began to realise that there was a side to Heaven that was purely functional. This was the business end of eternal life in the House of the Lord. The Registration Office needed to be like every other office block, because it worked the same as every other office. Death led Reg to the reception desk, where a plump female Angel sat smiling.

'Soul number RP-146241, Reginald Hallsworth,' recited Death.

The plump Angel looked down at her computer.

'Office sixty seven b, up the stairs, turn to the left, second door you come to.' She emphasised her directions with hand motions.

Reg couldn't take his eyes off her, she actually had wings, feathery wings, just like in the pictures he had seen. He knew Death was busy, shuffling though papers as he led the way to office sixty seven b, but he had to ask.

'Will I get wings like that?'

'Not as an entry level Soul,' Death answered, without looking up.

'Oh,' said Reg despondently.

Death registered the disappointment in Reg's voice. He felt sorry for him, he'd had a rough day.

'You can take a course to become an Angel. It's a lot of work mind. Most Souls don't bother, they just want to enjoy their time here, but every now and then someone wants to *put something back in*.' Death highlighted his last remark with a sarcastic inverted commas gesture.

Reg really fancied the sound of becoming an Angel. 'How long does it take?'

'Oh, only about couple of hundred years,' said Death nonchalantly.

The way Death had casually said *only* a couple of hundred years, made Reg realise that this whole eternal life business was going to take some getting used to.

Office sixty seven b was like, well, it was like every other office Reg had been to in his life, and his afterlife for that matter. The Angel in charge of Reg's registration would have been close to retirement had it not been for the whole immortal, eternal life thing. He had grey hair, in the last stages of receding before the term became baldness, and wore a pair of half rim spectacles, which he balanced half way down his nose.

'Papers please,' he said, in a slightly nasal voice.

Death dutifully handed over several sheets of paper, which the clerk began stamping and filing away.

'The Confirmation of Death Certificate appears to be missing,' said the clerk, whilst rummaging though the remaining papers.

'Probably dropped down the bottom of my briefcase,' replied Death, in way of apology.

Death began to search his briefcase, hunting for the missing paper. As the minutes ticked away his search became more and more desperate. It wasn't long before the entire contents of his briefcase were scattered on the desk.

'If you can't find the Confirmation of Death then I can't register him,' sighed the clerk with growing impatience.

'But, but, I wouldn't be here if I wasn't dead,' protested Reg.

'You might be pretending to be dead,' suggested the clerk.

'Why would I pretend to be dead?'

'Trying to get a sneak peak of Heaven, happens all the time.'

In fact, people rarely pretend to be dead in order to gain access to Heaven. Pretending to be dead is usually more closely associated with trying to hide from gangsters you owe a lot of money to or, more commonly, insurance fraud. Ironically, such actions are more likely to gain you access to Hell rather than Heaven. But the clerk shouldn't be criticised for his assumption, as after all, he was only doing his job.

Reg began to realise that the inner workings of the offices in the afterlife, were the same as every other office; full of red tape.

'I must have left it at home, I'll just go and get

it.' Death finally conceded.

'Fine, but you can't leave him here,' said the clerk, pointing to Reg with his pencil.

Death led Reg out of the office and back down into the reception area.

'Look, don't panic,' said a panicky Death. 'But I'm going to have to leave you in Purgatory, while I pop home and get your Confirmation of Death.'

'You haven't lost it, have you?' accused Reg.

It had been a bad enough day for Reg as it was. What with his life ending and everything. But not being able to start his death, that was a real inconvenience.

'Of course I haven't,' answered Death.

Incidentally, the term, of course, is most often used as an opening to a sentence which is a lie. Professor Cobblers identified the use of the phrase *of course* as a delaying tool, whilst the brain collates a suitable lie in response. For example, "you do love me, don't you?" "Of course I do." Death didn't know he was lying at this point, he just used the term *of course* in case he was. Reg's next question was more of a request than a question.

'Do I have to go to this Purgatory place? Can't I come with you?'

Death liked Reg, but not enough to invite him back for tea and biscuits. Besides, even though Death believed they could be friends (Reg would fit in great with the boys on poker night) the Department of Human Transition strictly forbade taking your work home with you. Death had already received a warning for doing that very thing, granted the circumstances had been slightly different. That had been when a plane had crashed carrying the contestants of the Miss Idaho Beauty Pageant. What a night that had been.

'Sorry Reg, department doesn't allow it.'

'Oh. So what is this Purgatory place?'

'It's mostly a Catholic thing, it's where they go

to absolve all their sins before entering Heaven,' explained Death.

'So why don't I have to go there?'

Reg knew himself well enough to know he wasn't exactly sin free. Nothing big, but definitely not totally sin free. Bill on the shop floor's stag night in Munich for one, that would definitely count against him.

'You're not Catholic,' said Death.

'But I'm going to Heaven, surely I've got to make up for my sins.'

'Look it's simple. Your religion has a lower entry requirement, so you get in. Had you been Catholic, then that night in Munich would have certainly counted against you.'

Death saw the shocked expression on Reg's face when he mentioned Munich.

'It's in your file,' explained Death, answering the question that he read on Reg's face.

'That doesn't seem fair on the Catholics.' Reg's sense of equality had been offended.

'I don't suppose it is really, but the alternatives would be even worse. It would mean everybody would have to follow one religion to have a shot at getting in Heaven.'

'That wouldn't be such a bad thing, there'd be a lot less wars for starters.'

'Yeah, but it'd also take away freedom of choice and freedom of choice is one of the greatest parts in the whole *gift of life* package. And what if you never came into contact with that religion? Would it be fair to send you straight to Hell for that reason?'

'I suppose not,' conceded Reg.

'No trust me, it's fairer this way. Entrance depends on whether, you've genuinely tried to live a good and moral life, so standards do vary between religions but it is the fairest assessment model to use. Anyway you of all people should approve, it's the only reason you scraped in.'

Reg was horrified by Death's last declaration. He had only just scraped in! It would be terrible waiting around to go to Hell right now. Death laughed to himself, Reg had sailed through the entrance assessment. He had always tried to do the best for his fellow man, and apart from a few moral grey areas had led an exemplary life. But hey, a bit of humility and self doubt was great for the soul.

'Welcome to Purgatory,' announced Death breaking Reg out of his inner turmoil.

Reg looked around. A second ago he'd been in an office block and now he was in Purgatory. He didn't think it was much of an improvement. The surrounding landscape was a mixture of bland beige and monotonous grey. The only sound was a low buzzing noise, like a monotone mumble, and the only scenery worth commenting on were featureless voids, and there were lots of them. Purgatory was boring.

'Okay, got to go,' declared Death.

'Wait, what do I do?'

'Just wait here, I won't be long. Oh and don't look like you're waiting, *they* hate people just hanging around here in Purgatory, especially when you're not a Catholic.'

'Wait, how do..?' Reg never finished his question. Death had gone.

Reg tried to look like he wasn't waiting around. He spent some time pretending to examine a featureless void, but you can only do this for so long. He couldn't see anyone around, despite the fact he knew *they* were watching him. Maybe he should pretend to be going somewhere, there was nowhere to head to, but he went there anyway. Then a panic struck Reg, what if he got lost wandering off nowhere? He might not be able to find his way back. The featureless voids would be no good in aiding his bearings. If he didn't do something *they* would know he was just hanging around and *they* might get nasty. Reg decided to travel so far towards nowhere, then pretend he'd gone the wrong way and go back, he could probably do this for a few hours before *they* noticed. As he walked, Reg listened more closely to the low buzzing noise. He realised it was the sound of chanting, thousands of droning voices repeating 'Hail Mary, full of grace.' He surmised that there must be a lot of minor sinners in the Catholic faith, but then, he thought, there's probably loads of minor sinners in every religion, it's just the Catholics had to atone for their sins. *They* would probably think it was strange that he wasn't joining in, so he joined in. He only knew the first part, but *they* probably wouldn't notice. And so it was that Reg spend the next few hours of his afterlife walking in circles, chanting 'Hail Mary's.' It's funny what *they* can make you do, when you think *they* are watching you.

Death was in a panic. He had arrived home over an hour ago and there still wasn't any sign of Reg's Confirmation of Death form. He had looked everywhere. This is a commonly used exaggeration. Had he in fact looked everywhere, he would have found the form. Death knew this, just like everyone else who uses it knows, but just like everyone else, he used it anyway. Quite obviously it wasn't in his house, and this could only mean one thing, he'd lost it. Death slumped onto his sofa. This would spell disaster for his career, he would definitely lose his Third Class status this time, he'd already received his final, final warning. On a plus side, he had found enough for a cup of coffee in foreign currency down the back of the very sofa he was sitting on; he couldn't believe it'd been there all along.

Death had to think of a plan. If he could just hide Reg for a few days, he could get a copy of the form sent out, nobody would be any the wiser. Death needed somewhere where Reg's presence could go undetected, and nobody would think to look for him, somewhere they would gladly take another soul.

'Where the hell am I going to find a place like that?' said Death out loud.

Despite his verbal tirade, it took Death another fifteen minutes hard thinking before the solution presented itself. Hell, I'll hide Reg in Hell. Hell was the perfect place to go.

Hell is rarely described as the perfect place to go, but for Death's purpose it did appear ideal. There were obviously a few loose ends that would need tying up, but the plan seemed solid. First, he'd need to get Reg into Hell, although they'll take anyone, there were still forms to fill in, and that would leave a paper trail straight to Reg, and Death's blunder. Luckily, the registration clerk in Hell owed Death a favour; he was sure he could get Reg in no questions asked. Secondly, and by far the biggest problem, was convincing Reg to go to Hell. Granted, it would only be for a couple of days, but Hell was not a popular destination amongst souls, most tried to avoid it at all costs. Death needed a bargaining tool. Maybe he could offer to get Reg on the Angel course, without going on the waiting list and with no entry exam. He was going to do that anyway when he saw how keen Reg had been to be an Angel; luckily he hadn't told him, it was going to be his parting gift (on occasion Death can be nice). He was sure Reg would go along with it, he was a good bloke, he'd cut Death some slack.

'No way, you can go to Hell,' objected Reg. (He hadn't intended the pun.)

'I probably will,' said Death in a disconsolate voice that he'd practised for just such an occasion.

There was little chance of Death actually going to Hell as a sinner *per se*, but he did have to go to Hell all the time in his line of work. He knew this statement would have been a bit misleading, but it wasn't a lie. Reg's sense of fair play got the better of him again. The thought of Death going to Hell for eternity because he wouldn't go there for a few days gnawed at his conscience.

'You sure it's only for a few days?'

Death sensed he was winning Reg over to his plan.

'Definitely. Few days max,' said Death earnestly. 'Really, Hell isn't as bad these days, I know a few people there. Okay, it's not pleasant, but you won't have to suffer any real torment, I promise.'

Most people know a few people in Hell, but Death knew people of influence in Hell, so he truly meant it when he said Reg wouldn't suffer. He was also telling the truth when he said Hell isn't as bad these days.

The popularity of Hell had never been great. However, it had taken a serious decline in the last millennium or so. This worried the top brass in the Underworld, so they decided to take action. They immediately employed some new, young and exciting advertising executives based in London to brainstorm the problem. The idea they came up with was based loosely on a model proposed by Dante in his controversial book *The Divine Comedies*. Dante's book suggested that Hell had levels; the greater the sin the lower the level of Hell you were placed in. The greater the sin, the greater the suffering you would endure. It was brilliant! It revolutionised Hell. Hell could open its gates with welcoming friendly smiles to all but the most serious sinners, monopolising the market for borderline evil souls. Suddenly, the number of souls opting for Hell rose. Statistics show Hell's popularity over the last few years has never been so high. Moral decline statistics have gone through the roof. The average person, when asked, will still say they would prefer to go to Heaven rather than Hell, but few have the conviction to go through with it. Hell will always be second in the ideal destinations surveys, but nevertheless, its numbers have risen significantly enough to justify the exorbitant price charged by the advertising executives.

'Okay,' agreed Reg, to Death's request.

'Brilliant, thanks, I owe you one.'

Death was genuinely overwhelmed that Reg had agreed. You had to be a really nice guy to go to Hell.

With a quick sharp click of his fingers Death summoned the elevator, bustled Reg inside and pressed the down button. Death wasn't going to give Reg time to change his mind. The elevator stopped with a *ping*. Death poked his head out and looked both ways to ensure there was nobody about and stepped out, indicating to Reg with a hand gesture to follow. In front of them was a red door, with a door mat on the floor, it read: Welcome to Hell.

'We're here,' announced Death.

As they walked through the door, Reg surmised that Hell was a lot easier to get into than Heaven.

Death greeted a Demon sitting at an ornate desk.

'Gurglemouth, my old friend.'

'Death,' acknowledged Gurglemouth.

Gurglemouth was an entrance administrator to Hell. His name was very apt, his mouth was surrounded by excessively large lips which dripped thick saliva, giving his speech a gurgling sound (it wasn't for this reason he was called Gurglemouth though. His parents had just liked the name). Gurglemouth's eyes were bulbous and a dull mustard yellow, giving him a toad like appearance, a look that was further enhanced by a slight green tinge to his skin. He was a particularly ugly Demon, even by Demon standards.

'Wat you want?' asked Gurglemouth.

'I need a favour.'

'Ask someone dat cares.'

'You owe me remember, that whole Judas thing,' reminded Death.

'Paid back, fardar Tobias you 'member, huh?'

Death had forgotten he'd used up that debt. 'Then I'll owe you a favour, how does that sound?'

'It sound good.' Gurglemouth gave a giggling sound as he spoke.

'I need a room for Reg here, just for a couple of days,' said Death, like he was booking a cheap hotel room.

'Wait 'ere. Be back now.' Gurglemouth left through a door behind him.

The door led to a large lavishly adorned room, with a roaring open fire. Bacchaus was sitting in a large red leather armchair when Gurglemouth entered.

'Wat I do?' asked Gurglemouth, bowing his head and avoiding eye contact with Bacchaus.

'Let him in,' commanded Bacchaus, in a deep rasping voice.

As Gurglemouth left, Bacchaus leant back, pressing his fingers together and placing his hands to his mouth. If you didn't know Bacchaus you would have concluded that he was praying, but Bacchaus certainly didn't pray, it was merely an outward sign that he was deep in thought. An innocent soul in Hell, how pleasant it would be to torment that one, he mused. But Bacchaus had little time for self indulgence, a particularly evil project he'd been working on was coming to fruition. Alas, all work and no play he thought in a moment of self pity, as even Demons feel pity sometimes. Sadly, it's usually for themselves.

Chapter 4

Norris was in Hell, not the kind of Hell he'd be in right now if he'd been the one on the receiving end of a big, blue Volvo estate, but an in the mind, I'm not really sure what to do, kind of Hell. Jenny had given Norris her number. You may think that doesn't sound like Hell, but you'd be wrong. It had all been so simple. Norris didn't even ask for it. She just handed it to him saying 'Here's my number.' The problem was just that, she didn't specify for what purpose she'd given him the number. Was it a "here's my number if an emergency comes up," kind of number? No matter how many times he ran back over the conversation in his head, he just simply couldn't remember her saying anything specific as to the purpose of the number. Had it been an invitation to arrange a date? Surely not, but what if it was? That created its own set of problems. When should he phone her? Too soon and he'd look sad, desperate, and possibly a bit obsessive and stalker-like, but then if he left it too late she may think he wasn't interested and find someone else.

She must have wanted him to call her, why else give someone your number? But then why would she be interested in him? If love had a league Jenny would be top of the highest division. Norris placed himself in a struggling low division team of part-time professionals. Although, occasionally low division teams played the best teams in cup ties. Often, talk of local boys becoming giant killers dominated the press, after an impressive one all draw in the first round. Sadly though, the top team usually demolished the part-timers in the second round, in a display of unrivalled skill, and never phoned or made any effort to stay in touch with the part-timers again. After two hours deliberation sitting next to the phone, Norris decided he would play Manchester United in a third round F.A. cup tie, and phone Jenny. Norris opened the folded piece of paper Jenny had given him. There was her number, and underneath she'd written in flowery handwriting :- call me if you want to meet up sometime, Jenny. Why hadn't she just said that in the first place? One-nil the part-timers.

Norris ran over how the conversation should go, before calling Jenny. 'Hi babes, it's Norris,' far too familiar. 'Jen, Norris here,' sounded like he was talking to a work colleague, too formal, but the first bit was good. Jen was better than Jenny or babes for that matter, but then she'd introduced herself as Jenny, maybe she didn't like the name Jen. Norris spent the next hour considering alternative opening sentences before he came to a conclusion. He'd text instead. Now what to text?

Jenny received a text late in the evening. "Hi Jen, hope you like the name Jen rather than Jenny." strange but cute she decided. "It's Norris, the guy at scuba class, just in case you know another Norris." She knew which Norris, but it was a valid point. "Just thought you might like to go out and do something, sometime." A bit vague, but that was nicer than some of the over confident guys she'd dated in the past. "Norris x" he'd put a kiss symbol on the end of the message but then she shouldn't read too much into it, text kisses were legendarily flippant. Everybody put text kisses on messages. It was for this reason that Norris had felt he could get away with putting a text kiss at the end of his message. Admittedly, it had taken him thirty seven minutes to finally come to that conclusion. It took Jenny thirty seven seconds to reply, "yeah sure, I'm free 2moz, tb wen u no wat u wana do. Jen x." Jenny figured she could get away with putting a text kiss on the end. It took Norris a further ten minutes to work out Jenny's reply, then he got it tb - text back.

Norris was faced with yet another dilemma. He wasn't well versed in the world of dating. He'd been on dates before, but he'd never really had to instigate one. Previously dates had always just seemed to fall into place. First thing in the morning Norris headed for the local bookshop. He was dressed normally, albeit a bit uncoordinated but he could easily pass for someone whose sanity had not recently taken a holiday in the Bahamas and left them at home.

The local bookshop was part of a large chain, that somehow managed to retain an almost rustic appeal. Its staff consisted, in the majority, of under paid students. Norris headed for the self help section. It was a large section. There must be a lot of people who need help out there he mused. The vast selection pleased Norris at first. Then he realised, he had to choose one. More than one book on dating seemed excessive, even for Norris. The first book he reviewed was *The Dating Way of Life by Al Marks*. At first it seemed promising but the author's claim that he had dated hundreds of different women, made Norris wonder why he'd had to date so many women if he was that good at dating. The next to be quickly rejected *Dating and Swinging* had an opening line 'Foursomes are the best way to date' which immediately put him off. The feeling was compounded by the fact that the only couple both Jenny and he knew were Tony and Liz. *Dates - Don't Bother - A single person's guide to living alone,* back on the shelf. *Dating the Man of your Dreams* unfortunately there didn't appear to be a *Dating the Woman of your Dreams*. He finally settled for a book by Dr. Nicola Stratham, (she was a doctor after all) and the title seemed promising; *Dating the First Step*. Its opening line also appealed to Norris. 'The trick to a successful date is spontaneity, spontaneity, spontaneity.' He decided to go home and read up on how to be spontaneous. In the queue for the till point Norris scanned through the bargain book sale bin. For some reason one book in particular caught his attention, *Is Your Sanity in Question?* He decided to buy it, for what reason he wasn't sure.

The book had been a recent addition to the book store. They had received an e-mail instructing them to place the book in clear view of customers purchasing their goods at the till. This was a common trick to increase sales of a particular book they had over ordered, but what was unusual was that they had been told to put it there, by someone called Jenny Angel in Head Office. No-one knew anyone called Jenny Angel in Head Office but they put them there anyway just in case.

According to Dr Nicola Stratham the key to arranging a successful date is to combine a meticulously planned and, if possible, previously tested venue or setting, with a spontaneous and adventurous new slant. Norris was confused by this. This had little to do with his dubious approach to sanity, it had more to do with the fact that he was human. As close as he could tell, it was comparable to putting marmalade on your toast (Previously tested) and then adding chopped liver (Spontaneous and adventurous). Norris tried his new recipe in an attempt to justify this approach to dating. This had little to do with the fact he was human, it had more to do with his dubious approach to sanity. Norris didn't like this approach to dating.

He began to wonder if *Dates - Don't Bother - A single person's guide to living alone* may have been the better choice. Nevertheless, he persevered with Dr Stratham and skipped to the end of chapter summary. 'Therefore, the successful date should encapsulate both. For example, dining out, but in a new venue, like the new Mongolian place that has opened down the high street. Whatever you choose as your date setting, always remember, be spontaneous.' Norris didn't know that new Mongolian place and it wasn't even in the phone book, so he decided to come up with his own spontaneous approach. Within an hour and a half he had devised two spontaneous approaches. First, arrange a date then not turn up. Although spontaneous, it had little benefit, as he would have to arrange another date and he'd be back to square one. So he decided to go with choice number two, arrange a date in that expensive restaurant all the girls in the office went on about, then change it last minute and take her ten pin bowling instead. Norris determined that Dr Stratham was a genius,Jenny would love it.

Jenny was excited and nervous, blissfully confused but most definitely happy, and all the other emotions you feel when you begin to fall in love. Although she was not falling in love, definitely not falling in love with a mortal, even if she did find him cute, funny and a bit geeky in a loveable way. Nevertheless, she could not help having a deep secret feeling that they would be like Romeo and Juliet and live happily ever after, (Jenny never really grasped the intricacies of Shakespeare).

Even Angels want to tell their girlfriends when they've got a date, and Jenny was no exception. At first Lucy had been a bit stoical about Jenny's announcement, then she erupted into a tirade of *he's wrong for you* speeches, then eventually she began to warm to the idea, especially, when she saw how excited Jenny appeared. Soon the two Angels were talking of the romance of forbidden or doomed love, and how the greater the obstacles that lay in their way the stronger their love would become. There was a practical side to Jenny's revelation, she needed an outfit, and Lucy was the queen of fashion and her kingdom lay within the borders of the Joan of Arc Boulevard. Lucy was a maestro, sorting through the various offerings the boutiques had on display, passing Jenny numerous combinations and accessories through the changing room curtains and instantly rejecting them, with insightful comments like 'makes your wings look big.' Not that Jenny would be revealing her wings on the date but she may want to double up on the outfit for another occasion, especially considering the price tags on clothes bought from the Boulevard.

After an exhausting day, Jenny had the perfect outfit for an evening out in La Trivoli, the expensive restaurant Norris had booked. Lucy had picked out a long white dress (they are Angels after all) with a split up one leg, a low cut sweeping front and an even lower cut back, strappy sandal style shoes, with a slight heel, and a silver necklace with a single white pearl, which finished the outfit off beautifully. Jenny viewed her outfit in the mirror, her hair was styled with a slight curl and falling down one side, and although coming dangerously close to a proclamation of vanity, she had to admit, Lucy was good.

Norris waited in the small coffee shop across the road from La Trivoli. He was wearing his best suit, not ideal for bowling but it added to the spontaneity of his date. The coffee shop would most likely have gone out of business years ago had it not been for the opening of La Trivoli. Almost overnight it became the standard meeting place for any people who wanted to enter the restaurant together, and as such, it was now able to charge premium rates for its adequate coffee. As Jenny walked in, every head turned. Norris stood up, and fought off two waiters who tried to pull out the seat for her.

'Sorry, I'm late. Have you been here long?' asked Jenny.

'No, five minutes max. You look wonderful.'

'I've never been to La Trivoli,' commented Jenny, little knowing that she never would.

'We're not going there. We're going bowling.' Norris played his trump card with confidence.

Jenny squealed with genuine delight and gave Norris a big hug.

'I love bowling!' exclaimed Jenny.

Your average high street bookies would have given low odds that Norris' choice of location for their date would have been received with some apathy. Few would have imagined that a Guardian Angel would list one of their favourite pastimes as ten pin bowling. However, Norris' haphazard choice had little to do with odds, it had more to do with luck, Norris had got lucky. Now those familiar with Norris' life would argue that this was at the very least highly improbable, he just didn't benefit from good luck, ever. However, the balance of luck is a precarious thing: remove a certain amount of luck from one individual and another will benefit. When Bacchaus removed a quota of luck from the unfortunate breakfast waiter he inadvertently transferred it to Norris. Therefore, it may be said that Bacchaus himself played an important role in instigating the perfect setting for Norris and Jenny's first official date. The irony of which was later to play on Bacchaus' every waking moment; through his own malicious nature he had heedlessly aided love. Bacchaus had acted as matchmaker to Norris and Jenny.

Jenny's excitement over the prospect of going ten pin bowling confirmed Norris' belief that Dr Nicola

Stratham was a genius. As they entered *Bowling Dome* Jenny looked around like a wide eyed child in a sweet shop.

'Can we have deep fried chicken and fries as well?' she asked.

Although this was hazardous to her diet, she justified her request with the knowledge that it wasn't everyday you got to go bowling and special occasions should allow a lapse in strict dietary regimes.

'Already ordered,' said Norris confidently, with a sophistication that only James Bond could have mustered.

Norris and Jenny walked over to the advanced booking desk. The assistant was a surly young woman, with a chewing gum disorder.

'Can I help you?' she said, pleasantly enough not to lose her job.

'Beachley, Norris Beachley.' Norris attempted to keep the Bond thing going.

'And?' enquired the assistant.

'Jenny,' replied a puzzled Norris.

'No. What time you booked?' responded the assistant, screwing up her face in a manner not really pleasant enough to keep her job.

'Oh. Eight thirty.'

Norris had lost the Bond thing, but Jenny hadn't noticed, she was in awe, watching a large overhead screen showing professional bowlers from America.

'You're lane twelve, you get your shoes from over there,' said the assistant waving her hand roughly in the direction of the shoe counter, and went back to reading her magazine.

'Come on, let's get our shoes,' said Norris to Jenny.

With much effort Jenny managed to tear herself away from the screen. In her opinion, there was only one thing better than watching ten pin bowling, and predictably, that was going ten pin bowling.

In marked contrast to the surly young woman at the booking counter, the assistant at the shoe counter was a surly young man. So far everything was going well. Norris had shown very few signs pertaining to his mental state until now.

'A pair of size nine bowling shoes, please,' requested Norris.

'I need your shoes.'

'Why do you need my shoes?'

'It's how we do it,' replied the assistant.

'I'm not giving you my shoes,' insisted Norris. They were his best pair afterall.

A young, pimply assistant manager appeared from behind Norris.

'Can I possibly help sir?' asked the assistant manager cheerfully.

'That man wants to take my shoes,' complained Norris.

'Yes sir.'

'Well I don't want to swap my shoes, mine are better.'

'You can have them back when you've finished bowling sir,' explained the assistant manager in an *understanding* manner.

'Promise?'

'You have my word sir.'

'Okay,' agreed a pacified Norris.

Norris passed his shoes to the surly assistant, who gave them an extra long spray with the spray can they keep behind the counter for particularly smelly shoes. Norris objected to the implication of this action, but decided not to say anything. Luckily, Jenny hadn't noticed the whole episode, she had problems of her own. Strappy sandals are perfect for dining in restaurants but not so ideal for taking off to swap for bowling shoes.

Lucy would have probably freaked out seeing Jenny wearing the bowling shoes with that dress.

She would most likely have ranted on about the whole look of her carefully picked ensemble being ruined, but Jenny didn't care. She was going bowling, what's more, she was going bowling with Norris. Even if he was a mortal, he was perfect. How many guys would take her ten pin bowling instead of going to an over priced restaurant? She put her hand in his as they walked to lane twelve, and wondered if he might even be willing to stay in and watch the football with a couple of beers every now and then, but surely that was asking too much.

As Norris walked with Jenny, he began to wonder if his life had really been that bad prior to his life changing epiphany. It appeared that all that was missing in his life was love, everything else he could cope with. Reluctantly he removed his hand from Jenny's grasp. It had begun to sweat, that was the effect she had on him, and sweaty hands were not conducive to bowling, or the James Bond image he was trying to establish. Although, Bond did perspire in *Goldfinger* when that laser was about to cut though his crotch, but hey who wouldn't. Whilst holding hands with a woman however, Bond did not get sweaty hands.

The atmospheric sounds of cheers, laughter and the distinctive crash of bowling balls knocking down pins filled the air, as Jenny demolished Norris in their first game. Jenny thought it was so cute of Norris to let her win, even though she had missed two strikes during the game. Norris thought how embarrassing it was that he couldn't even get one strike. Their food arrived shortly after their first game, a deep fat delight of overdone chicken and soggy fries all presented in a plastic basket trimmed with some type of frilly grease proof paper. As she tucked in, Jenny decided that La Trivoli would never have delivered such wonderful cuisine.

All too soon it was time to leave. Jenny couldn't believe he'd let her win all three games. Not only that, he'd thrown some really embarrassing shots just to make her laugh, her favourite being the time his ball had bounced over to the next lane. He'd even pretended he hadn't meant to, saying 'it was because the chicken had made his hands greasy.' Jenny decided it was by far the best date she'd ever been on.

Norris however, was feeling the pressure as they waited for Jenny's cab. The date had gone well, but now he felt the inevitable dilemma of whether to approach the first kiss. Jenny had kissed him before, but that had been in a more friendly way, not that he wasn't intending to kiss her in a friendly way, just a little bit more friendly than previously. He wanted nothing more than to kiss her but how do you make the move for the first kiss? He hadn't read that far into Dr. Stratham's book. As her cab pulled alongside them Norris decided to take decisive action.

'I had a great time, thank you,' he said offering his hand.

Norris decided to take the decisive action of being too scared to attempt that first kiss.

Jenny wasn't as good at taking decisive action, so she just kissed him instead. They shared a reasonably long soft kiss on the lips, just right.

As Jenny waved goodbye from the departing cab, Norris picked himself up from the floor, then sat back down on the curb. Wow! He wanted to dance, to sing, to shout out, he also wanted an umbrella, it had started to rain, but that didn't matter, he'd just kissed an angel sent down from Heaven. Not that he knew he had just kissed an Angel sent down from Heaven, but nevertheless he had.

It was a long walk home, but Norris decided to take it anyway. Despite the few spots of rain, it didn't seem as if there was going to be a heavy shower. A lot had happened to him over the last few days and he wanted to take some time to reflect on events. The only event that he actually reflected on during his walk, was Jenny. Maybe this was what life was about after all, not finding sunken treasure but finding love. He found himself greeting everyone he passed on the streets, most ignored his factual renditions of 'evening,' some smiled, but most frowned, he supposed they were still looking for their sunken treasure.

Perhaps the most notable of encounters Norris experienced during his walk, was a group of would be muggers, suitably attired in hooded tops, to enable the tabloids to run the title - hoodie gang. Fortunately, according to the press, all teenage troublemakers wear hooded tops which makes them invariably easy to spot and therefore avoid. However, Norris didn't know this and greeted them with a 'good evening lads.' The effect was remarkable, the hooded thugs returned his greeting albeit mumbled and walked off. A witness to this occurrence may have thought that *there must be a Guardian Angel looking after him*, but there wasn't, he'd put her in a taxi and sent her home half an hour ago.

Norris eventually arrived home, a bit wet but generally unscathed and happy. He was far too awake to sleep, so he decided to take a book with him to bed. He faced two immediate choices; *Dating the First Step* and *Is Your Sanity in Question?* Norris figured that he'd learnt all he needed to know about dating, the night's success had proved he was a master in the dating world, so he opted for *Is Your Sanity in Question?* As is commonly the case, sleep slowly sneaked up on Norris, (sleep rarely hides behind a counter and jumps out at you in a dramatic surprise kind of way) and he drifted into a peaceful slumber. His last conscious thought being provided by the book. Apparently, under certain circumstances it's okay to talk to God, it is less acceptable however, if God answers you back.

Chapter 5

Gurglemouth re-entered the room and took his seat.

'I call guide, he enter now. Agreed?' He turned to Death for a reply.

'Yes, excellent.'

Excellent was not a word Reg would have used to describe his pending entry into depths of Hell. Gurglemouth leant forwards and banged a small gong that was situated to the far left of his desk. There was an immediate puff of smoke, which predictably smelt of sulphur, and a fat-cheeked Imp appeared, coughing slightly.

Imps are generally considered in the Underworld as a lower class of Demon and are therefore employed in more menial tasks. Imps are easily recognisable, they never grow over four foot tall, have small horns on their heads, forked tails, and are red. It is for this reason that you will rarely hear the words 'he may have been an Imp, but I'm not sure.'

'Ugrat, you show him, where he go,' commanded Gurglemouth.

'Sure thing boss,' replied Ugrat in a voice that sounded similar to a deep baritone after inhaling a balloon full of helium.

Ugrat turned to Reg, smiling. (Imps also have small, sharp pointy teeth).

'Come with me,' said Ugrat. Then looking down. 'What no bags? It's a long stay you know. Little joke, make you laugh, yes?'

Reg looked back at Death with a nervous glance, like a small child leaving their mother for the first time at the school gates. Death gave him a wave forward and an encouraging smile, similar to the mother's response: At last a few hours peace.

Ugrat led Reg through a door opposite the one he and Death had entered. After a few paces down a nondescript corridor they came to a gate with a sign - Beware of the Dog. At the side of the gate stood an over sized dog kennel, the name Cerberus written above it. Reg remembered tales of a three headed dog that guarded the Gate of Hades. Ugrat saw Reg's inspection of the kennel.

'You no worry bout silly pooch, he gone for walkies. Besides he bark worse than he bite.'

Ugrat pulled out a key from his loin cloth and opened the Gate of Hades.

'Don't worry, Hell not so bad for you. You just guest,' comforted Ugrat.

'Thanks.'

'Besides you very short, me think you may be part Imp, no?' Ugrat tilted his head around to look at Reg's bottom. 'You sure you got no tail? Little joke, yes.'

The corridor beyond the gate began a steep decline. Stifling heat rose from the depths and the walls appeared to sweat with a clammy moisture.

'This nothing, you should be here mid-summer,' commented Ugrat.

I shouldn't be here at all thought Reg, but best make the most of it. He was British after all.

Suddenly, Reg realised he was extremely hungry. He hadn't eaten since he'd died and his body ached; he had walked for miles. Hunger, pain, and a reasonable amount of suffering are the staple products of Hell, without which Hell would be just another place you once went. It would be like Italy without its Renaissance art work, Florida without its water slides, and France without its arrogant waiters. It nevertheless came as a shock to Reg that he should feel the way he did. It wasn't that he hadn't previously been hungry or exhausted from his day, it was just that prior to his entry to Hell he had not been subjugated to the negative effects of such conditions. Now suddenly the enormity of everything that had recently happened to him began to weigh heavily on his shoulders. As Ugrat led Reg further down into the depths of Hell wave after wave of searing heat greeted them from the lower catacombs of the most unholy of places, taking Reg's breath away and stealing the moisture from his throat.

'How much further?' croaked Reg.

'Oh we pass your place, thought you'd like to see sights.'

'What?' said Reg in an outraged but too exhausted to do anything about it kind of way.

'Little joke, yes. Not far now, that it there.' Ugrat pointed ahead.

Ahead of them was a bridge and beyond that Reg could just make out the outlines of what appeared to be a town, of sorts.

'The Bridge of Lost Souls,' announced Ugrat.

Reg had become more than accustomed to the over dramatic titles given to landmarks that the afterlife, and in particular Hell, used. He wished just once someone would announce a Buttercup Hill or a Primrose Bridge. Still he had to admit, The Bridge of Lost Souls was an apt name. The bridge spanned a wide crevasse, tendrils of smoke rose from the depths of the deep abyss below wrapping their ethereal arms around the bridge. Reg couldn't help feeling that they were searching for him, waiting to pull him into the darkness below. It gave him the creeps. Hell was definitely a spooky place. The screams of thousands of souls echoed through the air as they rose from the tormented depths. Their pitiful pleas would never reach the Heavens, they'd had their chance, and quite frankly they'd blown it.

'Gotta pay bridge toll. You got change?' asked Ugrat.

'This is a toll bridge? Little joke, right?'

'No, no joke this time. This is Hell, you pay for everything in Hell.'

Reg had once heard of an old superstition where money was gently placed over the eyes of the dead. Apparently it was to help pay for the Ferryman's charge on the River Stix. Guess they went and built a bridge instead, he thought to himself.

'Ugrat pay for you,' offered the Imp.

'Thanks.'

The toll guard was at least eight foot tall, but other than that looked like any other toll booth worker; he looked bored.

'One and a half,' said Ugrat confidently.

'You're not a half, you're an Imp,' objected the toll guard.

Grumbling, Ugrat paid full price. That was the trouble with being an Imp, everyone recognised you as such.

Ugrat and Reg entered the town. The town was like any other in Hell and unlike any other on Earth. The residential areas were similar to high-rise flats, the main difference being that they had no fronts; leaving the residents exposed to all the outside elements. Ladders rose up the front fascia to give access to the apartments. From a security perspective this was a bad move, particularly in view of the fact that one in three of your neighbours was a hardened criminal.

The industrial area sent smoke billowing into the air from its tall chimneys, causing a heavy cloud to hang slovenly over the town, bathing it in a myriad of colours; from dull grey to dull green, with the odd tinge of dull yellow. The aroma that pervaded throughout was a combination of smells that you generally try hard to avoid throughout your life, an overpowering mixture of rotting meat, sulphur, and body odour on an industrial strength level. Reg found himself suffocating as the stench corrupted his lungs, taking his breath away. It reminded him of the perfumery counter at the local department store.

The shops were more a ramshackle of market stalls constructed from corrugated iron and plastic sheeting. There was no sense of uniformity amongst the stalls. The proprietors appeared to just set up shop where they felt like, and their rubbish and waste products lay scattered amongst them. One stall owner carefully bagged up his rubbish and placed it neatly to the side of his stall. An Imp immediately appeared with a long thin stick and began beating the stall owner until he ripped open the bag and kicked the contents over the street. The Imp gave him one last whack and disappeared.

'There's always one who breaks the rules,' said Ugrat, with a knowing nod.

'Surely it'd be better if everyone did things like bag their rubbish.'

'You be wanting recycling next,' giggled Ugrat. 'This is Hell, it not supposed to be better.'

'Yeah well, I still think...' began Reg.

Ugrat quickly pushed him to one side as a small eruption of flame burst from the ground where he was standing.

'What the...?' asked Reg.

'You should watch out, yes. See smoke?' Ugrat pointed to a spot further down the street, where a small column of smoke rose.

Suddenly a burst of flame appeared where the smoke had been, singeing a passer-by. Ugrat gave a mischievous laugh as the pedestrian yelled out.

'It funny, yes. Maybe I let you get toasted next time, no?' said Ugrat, still laughing.

Reg wasn't sure what to make of the Imp, Ugrat. Although he had saved him and did seem friendly enough, he also realised he would have happily watched him *get toasted* if he hadn't been a guest.

'Here you go, you stay here. Up that ladder you

live.'

Reg looked at the ladder. It rose twenty feet up one of the high-rise buildings to what Reg rightly assumed was his accommodation.

'Me see you later, got busy work to do now,' said Ugrat as he vanished in a sulphur smelling puff of smoke.

Reg climbed the ladder and found himself in a sparsely furnished room, with a bucket, and a wooden pallet for a bed. He slumped on the bed and despite the conditions began to doze. No sooner had Reg begun to drift off to sleep, when he woke with a start. A head had appeared at the top of the ladder, staring at him through a stocking mask.

'Sorry, didn't mean to wake you,' apologised the would-be burglar. 'I'll call back when you're not in.'

He gave Reg a wink and disappeared back down the ladder. Regardless of his trepidation, Reg began to doze again. It had been a long day since his death. People often describe the deceased as sleeping, so far, from Reg's own experience it was anything but the truth.

The would-be burglar appeared again.

'Still awake? Just checking, won't bother you again.'

'Get out.'

'Sure thing Guv, good as gone.'

The burglar ducked back down the ladder, a second later he popped his head back up again. Reg grabbed the bucket and threw it, catching the burglar on the side of the head. With a clatter he fell down the ladder.

'Okay, I'll call round later then,' came a voice from below.

Finally, to the atmospheric sounds and smells of Hell, Reg fell asleep.

Death was concerned. He knew Reg would be safe

in Hell for at least couple days but he didn't trust Gurglemouth; he'd been too eager to accept Death's proposal. Something wasn't quite right. It was like playing cards with the Four Horsemen of Everyday Life, you knew you had the better hand, but you also knew Negligence would cheat and ultimately win, and Death felt that somehow Gurglemouth was cheating. Death liked to think of himself as a bit of a psychic. Most people who think they're psychic say they have a sixth sense about death. Death however believed he had a sixth sense about people, and for some reason he didn't trust Gurglemouth.

The fact that Gurglemouth was a Demon may have had an influence on Death's psychic ability, as Demons are generally not regarded as the most trustworthy of beings. Whether through astonishing psychic ability or just plain common sense, Death decided to get Reg out of Hell as soon as possible.

Death returned to his office, quickly filled in the request form for Reg's Confirmation of Death and sent it off with the whistling mail boy who just happened to be doing his rounds as he finished. Death leant back in his leather swivel chair, he would have Reg tucked up in Heaven by Monday. He mentally congratulated himself. When he put his mind to it he was still a high flyer. He crumpled up a bit of scrap paper into a rudimentary ball, and tossed it at the waste paper basket.

'He shoots he scores!' he exclaimed, spinning in his swivel chair.

The fact that the makeshift basketball bounced off the rim and fell on the floor next to the bin held little significance to Death, but then psychic ability is like that.

Bacchaus sat in his red leather armchair, staring around his lavishly adorned office, when there was a knock at his door.

'Come in Gurglemouth,' he instructed.

Gurglemouth reluctantly entered, trying to avoid eye contact, his toad-like face sweating profusely. Gurglemouth hated coming into this office. His bulging eyes quickly glanced at a lamp shade on the desk, the face of his predecessor had been used to decorate it. Bacchaus was legendarily swift and harsh with his punishments for any of those that displeased him.

'I want the Imp Ugrat to work a double shift,' instructed Bacchaus. 'And ensure that he visits our guest before his shift is over. I'm placing Ugrat in charge of his welfare.'

'It done, Sire. Is dat all?' asked Gurglemouth hesitantly.

'You may go.'

Gurglemouth held in his sigh of relief as he headed towards the door.

'Oh, one other thing,' said Bacchaus casually.

Gurglemouth knew better than to pay heed to Bacchaus' casual tones.

'Yes my Lord?'

'That Father Tobias incident, we will be talking.'

'Yes, Sire.' Gurglemouth's black heart sank.

Gurglemouth left the office, closing the door behind him, he slumped on the floor and pulled at his skin wondering what upholstered furniture Bacchaus would make out of him.

Bacchaus glanced at his foot stool, it was getting a bit worn.

Reg awoke from a pleasant nightmare to the harsh realities of Hell. The feverish beads of sweat that his tormented slumber had produced quickly evaporated in the intense heat of the Underworld. He opened his eyes, then quickly shut them again tightly, in a vain attempt to regain his sleeping status and resume his dream. Being chased down a street by a mob of Imps trying to drag him back to

Hell (which strangely enough had been situated on Earth, a sort of prison) would have been under other circumstances, a less appealing alternative. But as the sounds and smells of Hell seeped into his consciousness Reg wished he was running for his life down Talbot Street. Finally, he gave up his struggle and opened his eyes fully.

His stomach began to rumble, then with a feeling although not wholly unique to Hell but nevertheless rare, he felt hope. He remembered he had a packet of boiled sweets in his pocket, maybe he had brought them with him to the afterlife. He reached down to his pocket. It was gone, someone had stolen his pocket! Looking down, to his dismay he realised that they'd also stolen the trousers he kept his pocket in. In fact, they'd stolen all his clothes apart from his white underpants that were slightly grey, not enough to declare them past their sell by date, but not quite new enough to call white anymore, and one shoe. Reg pondered why the thief had left one shoe, particularly since they had taken the trouble to remove the sock from the very same foot. Then it occurred to him, he was looking for a one legged thief, a left legged thief to be precise. The sock could obviously be doubled up to suit either foot where the shoe could not. Pleased with his deductions he allowed himself a small yell of frustration.

It was at that moment that Ugrat decided to pay a visit. As the puff of sulphur smelling smoke cleared, Reg looked up at the Imp, he instantly recognised him. Ugrat took a moment looking Reg up and down.

'I see One Legged Frank visit you too,' said Ugrat.

'I knew it!' exclaimed Reg. A one legged thief. His deductions were right. Poirot may be from Belgium, but he couldn't have done better.

Ugrat slumped down on the make shift pallet

bed next to the still prone Reg.

'Me beat dead,' sighed Ugrat in an exhausted voice.

'You mean deadbeat.'

'No. Me beat dead, with a big stick. Lot and lot of punishment to give, work double shift when don't want to.'

'Well it's your choice to work a double shift,' said a still slightly disgruntled Reg.

Although Reg would have normally sided with the workers his current mood was not particularly sympathetic after the robbery.

'No choice gives us, boss says work, we work. No breaks, just work. No fun being an Imp.'

'What do you mean? Haven't you ever heard of workers rights?'

'Boss have all the rights, none left for workers.'

'That's ridiculous!' said an outraged Reg.

Those unfamiliar with Reg's Earthly personality would question his sudden outburst and change of approach. Those familiar would just sigh and say 'oh no, here we go again'. Ugrat found his response confusing but was quite pleased that someone was interested in the hardships he suffered. So he continued telling Reg all his woes in the workplace, quite simply working in Hell was, well, hell. As the Imp listed his grievances, Reg the trade unionist began to formulate a plan of action. He would become a crusader, battling for the rights of the workers of Hell, the poor downtrodden honest working men, no wait, the honest working Demons.

It could be argued that Reg's sympathies at this point were slightly misplaced. Certainly the Imps do receive a raw deal in their working environment, but they are in fact far from innocent. Many of the hardships suffered by mankind are instigated by Imps. Not the big stuff, that's generally the domain of greater Demons, but those little annoying things: It's the Imps that ensure that bread always falls butter side down. It's the Imps that phone when you're in the bath, and hang up with a withheld number just as you get there. And, it's the Imps that feed pigeons laxatives, just as you finish polishing your car. Nevertheless, Reg felt that they deserved a better deal and the only reasonable way to achieve this... Strike action!

Chapter 6

Gurglemouth gently rubbed the skin on the back of his hand. He liked his skin, okay so it wasn't the best skin, it had a dull green tinge and was a bit loose in parts, but he liked it. The main reason he liked it, the overriding factor, more important than any other reason, was because it was attached to him. He was almost certain this wouldn't be the case for much longer. Something had happened in Hell during the night, something bad. Something bad happening in Hell may not seem an unusual occurrence, but on this particular occasion it was. This something bad was not directed at the *innocent* souls condemned there, (no-one admits to being guilty in Hell) this something bad was directed towards the Demons who ran Hell. And now Gurglemouth had to bring the news to Bacchaus.

Bacchaus was not the sort to *shoot the messenger*. He was more the sort to flail the skin off the still-living messenger, use said skin to upholster any threadbare furniture he had lying around, flick salt and vinegar crisps at the exposed flesh of the messenger until he got bored, and then shoot the messenger. Gurglemouth didn't like being the messenger.

Gurglemouth paused before lightly tapping the door to Bacchaus' office. Of course, he considered running away and not delivering the message, but Bacchaus treated those who failed to deliver a message really badly.

'Enter,' came a response from the other side of the door.

'Fraid got bad news, Sire,' said Gurglemouth entering the room. 'It de Imps... dey've... dey've.'

'Yes? Out with it.'

'Dey've gone... gone on strike!' Gurglemouth fell to the floor in a blubbering mass.

Demon Bacchaus stroked his chin thoughtfully, he already knew the Imps were on strike, it was just what he had expected after letting such a staunch trade unionist into Hell. Nevertheless, he carefully studied the messenger's skin; green. He looked around his office, he quite liked the red theme he had established and green was so last season. He knew you should never mix seasons, one of those mind numbing daytime interior design programmes he had personally commissioned had said so. His mind wandered to his success in promoting such soul destroying television.

In one foul swoop he encouraged envy, for all those things the viewers didn't have; greed, for wanting the things they saw on such programmes; and general despair at the realisation that they'd spent the whole day watching such soul destroying television. As an added bonus, he had created a mass market for false idol worship. Instead of applauding people of true greatness and good deeds, people now held the lowest, most insipid and self serving souls in highest regard - the celebrities. How great to live in an age where women who regularly flaunted their size double "F" breast implants could be held in greater regard and higher esteem than those who spend their whole lives caring for orphaned children.

Gurglemouth's blubbering broke his happy thoughts.

'Go!' commanded Bacchaus. His recent musings had placed him in a good mood, he'd let the messenger live for now.

Gurglemouth tripped over his own feet in his haste to leave the room. He couldn't believe he still had his skin.

Reg's rousing call for strike action had received overwhelming support. The Imps had voted in favour of direct action with a unanimous three to one. Okay, so three to one in favour wasn't exactly unanimous but when it comes to voting no-one ever really counts, it's only the result that's important. Besides, he was quite sure that the few that did vote against him had misheard or not heard at all, it was an extremely large crowd he had addressed earlier. Ah, his speech, it had been his crowning glory:

'Friends, fiends and fellow denizens of the Underworld, lend me your ears and other various appendages you use for listening. Too long have you suffered under the cruel yoke of the demonic bourgeoisie. Too long have you, the slightly less than honest workers of the Underworld, toiled without reward. Too long...'

'... Is your speech. We gonna strike or wat?' Interrupted an Imp near the front.

'Who wana strike?' interjected Ugrat.

Reg's words had obviously struck a chord with the Imp masses. As a cacophony of voices erupted, the vote came in. The Imps were on strike. Had he not been dead, this moment would have stayed with Reg for the rest of his life.

Reg now stood next to an old oil drum with a few broken planks of wood burning in it. He was at the head of the picket line. Around him stood numerous Imps carrying plaques proclaiming their demands. One such banner read: A fair day's evil doing - for a fair day's wage. Granted it wasn't the catchiest of slogans but it got the message across.

It took the tortured souls the best part of the morning to fully grasp what was happening. After a few tentative acts of general pleasantries went unpunished (the perpetrators looking fearfully over their shoulders), the occupants of Hell began to act positively saintly. They began greeting each other with smiles and good mornings, clearing up rubbish that had been lying around for decades, and even trying to make amends for previous wrong doings. By lunchtime *all hell was breaking loose* in Hell. Even One Legged Frank turned up at the picket line to return Reg's clothes. Although, to his dismay Reg realised that the packet of boiled sweets were no longer in the pocket of his trousers. At that moment Ugrat appeared next to him, with his customary puff of smoke.

'You still here, yes?' questioned Ugrat.

'Of course. This is a strike.'

'How long strike take?'

'Till the bosses make an offer. That's when I negotiate for you. With the Devil himself I guess.' Reg gulped at this last prospect. He hadn't really thought that far ahead.

'Devil not in charge of Hell, oh no. He too busy with matters on world, yes.'

'Oh. Then who's in charge?' asked Reg, feeling slightly relieved.

'That be Dark Angel Bacchaus,' said the Imp, his voice dropping to a whisper. 'He's abaddon.'

'He's a what? A badun?'

'Yes, yes. That what I say,' replied Ugrat looking nervously around.

'Oh right, a bad un,' said Reg nodding as he comprehended what the Imp was saying.

'Yes, he's a bad un.'

'Well he hasn't dealt with the negotiating skills of Reginald Hallsworth yet. I can be a bad un too!' said Reg, pulling his recently reacquired trousers high up his waist.

Chapter 7

Death looked in the mirror. Most people boasted about the times when they had *looked death in the face,* but he took this kind of thing in his stride. Damn, he looked good. This was it. This was the beginning of the new Death. Well in fact, the return of the old Death, the go-getter Death of before. Today would mark the beginning of a new life for Death. He was going to pick Reg up from Hell, relocate him to Heaven, sort out his desk, take a light lunch and then... then the all new efficient Death would shake up the whole department. Oh yes, he was going to be back on track for that promotion to Second Class. He licked his index finger, brushed it across his eyebrow, and then pointed it at his reflection simultaneously making a clicking noise. He left for the office, hand in hand with his new found confidence.

As Death strode through the office, everyone looked at him and promptly got out of his way. He surmised they must recognise his new go-getter attitude and knew he was too busy to partake in his usual morning chit chat. Some even dived under their desks, papers and documents flying in the air with their haste. A bit of an extreme reaction to take, he thought, but hey, they weren't disrupting his new machinations. The new Death used words like machinations.

At his desk, his computer innocently flashed a warning that a memo was awaiting his attention. It's hard to believe that a computer could do anything *innocently,* without some ulterior motive involving world domination and the such. But nevertheless, Death's computer flashed innocently, its time would come, but not today, not now, but soon, oh yes its time would come. Death casually clicked the button to call up the memo and leant back in his chair. He suddenly sat up. Memos usually involved topics of: Can we cut down on the amount of staples/paper/ink/pens being used, or some idiot from the fourth floor jumping off or out of something for charity. This memo was different. This memo came from the top, and was calling him into the conference room for an emergency meeting. It could mean only one thing... promotion! The heads of Human Transition must have recognised his new go-getter attitude, not bad considering he hadn't even put any of his ideas into practice yet.

Death made his way up to the conference room and gave a light musical tap on the door. 'Enter' came a hollow response, and he pushed through the door with a flourish. He entered the room with confidence. Unfortunately, confidence suddenly realised it had a more important place to be and promptly left. Death wasn't facing the smiling faces of a promotion board. He was facing the scowling faces of a disciplinary board. The upturned corners of his smiling mouth began to feel the weight of impending doom and started to droop. It could mean only one thing. They'd found out about Reg. Deny everything, deny everything, they couldn't possibly have any proof, just deny everything. Death's eyes caught the guiltily smiling face of Reg, standing to one side. Okay, new plan, admit to your mistake and hope for the best.

The disciplinary board consisted of four members:- Archangel Michael, Head of Heaven and head of the disciplinary board. He had a reputation of being tough but fair. When Satan had been an Angel and had broken the rules, it had been Michael who beat him up and cast him out of Heaven, tough but fair.

Susan Pendridge, a skinny women with a long

pointy nose. She was head of Human Transition and despite her businesslike manner had always had a soft spot for Death. If he had anyone on his side it would be her.

Draco, the infamous ancient Athenian scribe who set down a series of common laws. The eponymous Draconian Laws were renowned for their harsh punishments (the majority of crimes held the death penalty). As justification Draco claimed 'it prevents minor crimes, and for major ones its the worst punishment I can think of.' Needless to say the presence of such a hard-liner did not bode well for Death.

The final member of the board went by the name of Ghandi. Although Death had never met Ghandi, his reputation as an all-round nice guy preceded him. His presence, along with Pendridge, gave Death a glimmer of hope.

'Thank you. You may leave now,' instructed Archangel Michael to a sixth figure standing in a shadowy recess near Reg.

'Glad to have been of service,' said a bowing Death 355 fourth class.

Death always hated Death 355, the brown nosing git had been after his job for years. As he left, he gave Death a smug little smile.

'Okay look I know I made a little mistake, but I've got Reg's papers here,' said Death indicating his briefcase. 'No harm done.'

Reg gave a little nervous cough. The board gave no response to Death's plea.

'Oh come on. I mean nobody's the wiser. Reg said he didn't mind, and now he can be placed in Heaven and everything can go back to normal.'

Silence. Death looked across to Reg, who quickly ducked his head down.

'What? What's going on?'

'I'm afraid everything is not going to be back to normal,' replied Archangel Michael.

'What have you gone and done?' asked Death in a suspicious manner, slowly turning back towards Reg.

'It was the working conditions of my comrades.'

'Your comrades?' asked Death slowly, fearing the worst.

'Er, yeah. My comrades the er, Imps.'

Death placed his hands over his face and gave a low muffled moan.

'I didn't really think the strike would cause that much of a problem.'

'The strike?' Death raised his head out of his hands for a brief moment, only to bury it deeper.

'And now perhaps you can grasp the problem that you have caused,' said Archangel Michael crisply.

'So how bad is it?' asked a forlorn Death.

'We've got souls queuing up with nowhere to go. Within forty eight hours we'll be overrun. Without open access to Hell the whole system will collapse,' explained the Archangel. 'I'm afraid it's a disaster of biblical proportions.'

Unfortunately, Archangel Michael was not prone to exaggeration. When he said *of biblical proportions*, he meant it. And he should know better than most, he'd witnessed most biblical proportion disasters, he'd even had his hand in a couple of locust plagues himself.

'You leave us no choice,' interjected Pendridge in her high whiney voice. 'I'm sorry Death. Hand in your scythe and cloak. Your service is no longer required.'

The scythe and cloak were purely ceremonial since the new look Human Transition Department had been brought into practice. These items did however represent a badge of office. Without these Death would no longer be Death. He would be just another soul without any true purpose, wandering endlessly in eternal limbo. It was bad.

'Wait,' pleaded Death. 'There... There must be something we can do. Reg can't you call off the strike?'

'When I found out about this, I tried to call off the strike. They wouldn't listen. They even called me a scab. Me, Reginald Hallsworth, a scab!'

'What about breaking the strike?' suggested Death.

'This proposal has merit,' concurred Draco. 'We could execute them all.'

'No, no.' It was Ghandi's turn to speak. 'Your reasoning is flawed. Without the workers Hell could not be reopened. This must not be the path we are travelling. In India passive resistance was being the key. Shaming our opponents into submission.'

'Passive resistance will do little to break this strike,' disagreed Archangel Michael.

'Passive resistance was but one of the many methods I was planning to break British rule in India,' continued Ghandi. 'Many many plans I was having. Perhaps turning to my back up plan.'

'What was that?' asked Death, excited at the prospect of getting out of this biblical disaster.

'We must be hitting them in the balls with a big stick,' insisted Ghandi.

'Er I'm not too sure...' said Pendridge.

'Yes, yes, hitting them in the balls with a big stick,' reasserted Ghandi. 'It is a most enlightened way.'

'Okay, why don't we put that idea on the back burner,' suggested Michael.

'Hit them in the balls with a big stick!' shouted Ghandi, standing on his chair.

'Sit back down,' requested the Archangel in a commanding voice.

'Okay. But we must be hitting them in the balls,' said Ghandi, sitting back down.

'Chill out Ghandi,' said the Archangel in a

calming voice. 'Our emotions are quite obviously running high. Unfortunately, we have little to no jurisdiction over the Underworld. So both Dracos' and Ghandi's solutions are unattainable.'

'Er. Can I make a suggestion?' asked Reg, raising his hand to speak.

'Of course,' granted the Archangel.

'Well I was involved in a strike action before, and the management, they were typical bourgeoisie tyrants I can tell you...'

'Yes?' said Pendridge as a way of hurrying him along.

'Well anyway, er, they didn't bother trying to break the strike, they just moved the business to another area. You could make a second Hell, you know, until the strike's over. Somewhere to keep the souls until all this is resolved.'

'This idea has real merit,' agreed Archangel Michael.

'Yes. But planning permission is so difficult to get now in the Afterworld,' complained Pendridge. 'We'd never get it for a second Hell.'

'Ah, yes pity,' concurred Michael.

Death saw Reg's proposal as his best chance of getting out of this mess and was reluctant to let it go so quickly.

'Planning permission is easy to get on Earth,' said Death. 'We could make a Hell on Earth.'

'Erm. I'm not too sure,' objected Michael.

'It would be perfect. People could see how bad Hell really is,' continued Death. 'It would be a proactive move against sin.'

'You know, I think we might have something here,' said Pendridge siding with Death. 'Are you telling me Michael, that Heaven couldn't do with a few more members? After seeing Hell nobody will want to sin.'

Archangel Michael sat for a few moments mulling the idea over, Death watching every muscle on his face. Eventually, the Archangel spoke.

'Okay, we'll go with it. We shall create Hell on Earth.'

The whole board gave themselves a clap.

'Pendridge, I'll leave the details to you.'

'Er. What about me?' asked Death.

'We will be needing someone to sort out the logistics, where to build *et cetera,*' said Pendridge, turning to Michael.

'Yes quite. Nobody's going to want that job.'

'I can do it!' said Death quickly, after a wink from Pendridge.

'Very well. You are however, on suspension until this matter is fully resolved,' warned Michael. 'If anything goes wrong, you will find yourself fully accountable!'

As Archangel Michael, Draco, and Ghandi left the conference room Pendridge turned to Death and Reg.

'Right. You two,' she said, adopting the tone of a headmistress facing two naughty children. 'You have caused a whole lot of trouble.'

Reg and Death both put their hands behind their backs and ducked their heads.

'You,' she said to Death. 'I have never known such irresponsibility. Leaving an innocent soul in Hell over the weekend, while you went out gallivanting. What were you thinking?'

'I just thought...'

'That's the problem. You didn't think!' She turned to Reg. 'And you! What gave you the right to cause so much pandemonium?'

'Sorry.'

'Well you will be sorry. Both of you,' said Pendridge continuing her tirade. 'Because both of you are going to sort this mess out pronto. Yes that's right, both of you!'

'But I thought I was going to Heaven now.'

'Well you thought wrong, didn't you Reginald.

This is as much your mess as Death's. And I hope you have some idea how you're going to implement this plan of yours.'

'Er...'

'Might I suggest you start by getting a human guide,' said an exasperated Pendridge.

'I was about to suggest that myself,' lied Death. 'We should get the most intelligent being on the planet.'

'That would be Boo Boo,' said Pendridge. 'Although, technically he's a monkey.'

'What? That's impossible. The most intelligent er, being on the planet is a monkey?' questioned Reg.

'Yes, but unfortunately he's busy at the moment. You'll have to find someone else yourselves.'

Despite Reg's shock, the most intelligent being on the planet is in fact Boo Boo the monkey. Boo Boo's rise in the intellectual field began with a simple premise made by a university lecturer. Fed up with his students' inability to conceptualise the vastness of infinity, he devised an example. Given an infinite amount of monkeys and an infinite amount of word processors, they would eventually write the complete works of Shakespeare. A particularly advanced student then questioned why they would choose to write something that had been written before? With a sigh the lecturer explained he'd only used Shakespeare as an example and it could be any book, the greatest book ever written, that explained the meaning of life and true happiness, such were the infinite possibilities of infinity. However, the lecturer never really fully considered the implications of such a statement. Following this premise, it would suggest that at some point, given an infinite amount of monkeys and word processors, one monkey with one word processor would write the greatest book ever written explaining the meaning of life and true happiness. Therefore, at any one point in time a monkey with a word processor could complete this work. On a Tuesday afternoon, Boo Boo the monkey wrote *Life Explained* on his owner's word processor.

Although far too complex for the general public's consumption, *Life Explained* was to cause world wide acclaim amongst the members of the intellectual world. It presented the idea that the secret to happiness lay in two directions at polar opposites. As someone achieved the one the other moved further away. Therefore, eternal happiness was in fact impossible. The book made Boo Boo's owner a fortune and sky rocketed Boo Boo's career. Unfortunately, Boo Boo's second book entitled *zzzbbks>,ssz!!!* wasn't such a success. Although, certain intellectuals claimed it was just far too advanced for mankind to understand.

'A monkey?' questioned an extremely puzzled Reg.

'Yes a monkey,' sighed Pendridge. 'Do you know anyone as intelligent as a monkey?'

Come to think of it Reg didn't know anyone as intelligent as a monkey.

'Do we really need anyone else anyway?' asked Death.

'It has to do with fair representation. According to Charter 361, a representative of interested parties must be present at any and or all, developments regarding or having direct impact upon their natural environment and or their way of life,' she explained. 'Besides, you two would probably get lost.'

'A monkey?'

'Yes Reginald, a monkey.'

Theologians also had the same problem as Reg was having, grasping the fact that the most intelligent being on the planet was in fact a monkey. Until that is, one pointed out that it was probably God's way of getting revenge on Darwin's theory of evolution. A monkey more intelligent than man disrupted Darwin's theory of the natural development of the species. If a monkey was a more highly developed being than man, then Darwin was wrong, his theory was wrong, and everyone who believed in his theory was wrong. Hah, that's egg on your face Mr Darwin, wrong, wrong, wrong! Oh revenge is sweet. Okay Scientologists you're next!

'So basically, we've got to find someone to accompany us on our travels around the world, find a suitable location for a new Hell.' Death took a deep breath. 'Report back with our chosen location within forty-eight hours, and I can keep my job?'

'That's about the crux of it, yes.'

'No problemo.'

'Good, I'll leave you to it then,' said Pendridge, picking up some files from the table in front of her and swiftly leaving.

'So, er, you know what we're going to do. Right?' said Reg, turning to face Death. 'I mean you've got a plan?'

'Not a clue,' said Death, with a smile.

'But you sounded so confident.'

'Well the way I look at it, when you're facing insurmountable odds and there seems like no way out, Death has the answer.'

'Oh, okay. So when this is all over, I mean when everything is back to normal, I get to go to Heaven right?'

'Absolutely.'

Remarkably, considering all that had happened to him, one look at Death's smiling face, and Reg felt like he could trust him. Death was a salesman.

'Look, I'm sorry about the strike, I didn't mean to get you into trouble.'

'Nah it's nothing. Bound to happen really.'

'So what we going to do then?'

'Well you'd better think of someone we can use as a guide.'

'But I don't know any monkeys, well not very well, and certainly not the responsible intelligent type.'

'It doesn't have to be a monkey, anyone will do.'

'What like, just a regular person?'

'Yeah, anyone.'

'I knew she was wrong about the monkey thing.'

Death let it pass, after all time was pressing and he could understand Reg's confusion. He'd had a lot to take in since his recent demise. Besides, the boundaries between slightly intelligent monkeys and humans had always been a bit blurry to him too.

'So anyone, anyone at all?' asked Reg.

'Yep.'

'Can't you choose?'

'I would, but everyone I meet are kind of dead. Bit of a barrier really, don't you think?'

'Yes, yeah of course.'

Slowly, like a trickle of leaking water from a dam wall which would eventually cause a massive breach and rain down terror and destruction on the innocent hard working village folk below, an idea began to form in Reg's mind.

'I get to choose anyone?'

'Yep.'

'I'd be able to physically touch them?'

'Yep.'

Death knew what Reg was thinking, this was his chance to see a loved one, to talk with someone he never got the chance to say good-bye to.

'It would probably be quite a shock for that person right, probably ruin their life, drive them insane?' asked Reg.

'Well, I suppose it would be quite a shock, but we could soften the blow.'

'No need. I've got just the person,' said Reg, with a slightly malicious grin.

Death decided he didn't know what Reg was thinking after all.

'Okay, let's get going then,' said Reg cheerfully, clapping his hands together.

The screams of the young family who moved into a house down stream of the dam went unnoticed.

Chapter 8

Jenny woke with a yawn, as is customary with those who have recently risen from a deep slumber and want to inform the rest of their body of this significant fact. Her yawn however, was interrupted somewhere between the *w* and the *n*. Her brain had fully awakened somewhere in the *a* part and was now reminding her of the previous night's events. At first the yawn was interrupted with an *oh* then a smile, but this gradually turned into a frown. She had kissed Norris. Although, a kiss is not generally perceived to be a binding contract, the emotion they both felt during the act did. The smile she bore was undoubtedly due to the fact that she did genuinely love Norris, and the kiss was her heart's desire. The frown was due to the fact that she did genuinely love Norris; a love that could never work. They were from different worlds (well technically they were from different planes of existence) and so, the restrictions that this created meant their love would never work.

The lovelorn Angel stumbled out of bed. Apparently, her left leg was still waiting for the *n* part of the yawn before waking up. The tangled emotions continued threading their twisted journey through her mind, clogging up other parts of her brain; those parts of the brain necessary for everyday survival, such as what to wear on your short excursion to the local shops. As a result, one hour later Jenny made her way to Shelley's Deli wearing a nice flowery blouse, a hand knitted scarf, jogging bottoms and knee high boots; a carefully created ensemble to portray an image of someone whose mind was elsewhere whilst getting dressed.

As if to prove that unfortunate twists of fate also occur in the afterlife as well as in mortal life, it was at this moment that fate chose to reintroduce two old Angel school friends.

'Four chocolate covered croissants please,' said Jenny, to the assistant at Shelley's Deli's counter.

'Jenny, is that you?' said an excited voice behind her.

She turned her attention from the savoury delights on offer and looked down at her attire. It was at this moment that the *fashion sense* part of her brain became untangled. Please don't let it be me, let it be another Jenny. She didn't mind her close friends seeing her dressed like this, but not someone she hadn't seen in ages. As she turned around her heart sank, it was Angel Katie.

Angel Katie had gone to Angel school with Jenny, and she had been one of the popular crowd. Not just one of the popular crowd, the most popular. The teachers loved her because she was the most intelligent in her year, the other female Angels loved her because she was the funniest and coolest in her year, and the male Angels loved her because she was also the prettiest Angel in her year. If this was a Hollywood movie Angel Katie would have been a bitch, and would have at some point got her comeuppance for being so horrible to Jenny. However, this was not a Hollywood movie and Katie had always been particularly nice to Jenny, and to everyone else for that matter. The bitch!

'Oh hiya Katie.'

'Jen, I haven't seen you in ages,' said the pristine looking Angel. 'You look...' Angel Katie looked Jenny up and down and gave a giggle. 'You look like your mind was elsewhere this morning. It's typical isn't it? It happened to me the other day. I went out in my slippers just to pick up some milk and ran into my ex Robert.'

In an instant she had made Jenny feel much better about her appearance, recognising this was not her usual dress sense and confessing to the same thing happening to herself. It was no wonder everyone liked her.

'What you doing around here?' enquired Jenny.

'On my way to work. Thought I'd pick up some bagels for the girls in the office.'

Girls in the office. Katie made it sound so ordinary, but Katie was a Vengeance Angel. The girls in the office weren't just ordinary girls in the office, they were Vengeance Angels too!

The Vengeance Angels have by far the best jobs in the Angel world. They are the best paid, and are essentially Angel celebrities. Not the kind of celebrities that open village fetes, but the kind of celebrities that get to open government buildings, hospitals, and sports stadiums. Katie had got into the Vengeance Angel Academy after graduating from Angel school. The odds of getting into the Vengeance Angel Academy were like those of winning the lottery. They only took the best of the best, then took the best of those and finally chose the best one they were left with. If getting into the Academy was like winning the lottery jackpot then graduating from the Academy was like winning the lottery jackpot without even buying a ticket.

She had graduated with flying colours, and joined the most famous Vengeance Angel team - Angel Force Three. Katie was an expert in fire and brimstone. The closest equivalent in worldly terms, would be an explosives expert. She was a dab hand at lightning strikes, fire storms and turning people into pillars of salt. The leader of the team was Angel Aimee. Her speciality was hand to hand combat. Angel Aimee had fought alongside Archangel Michael when he had thrown down Satan and his followers from Heaven. Aimee still looked incredibly good for her age, maybe mid-twenties, which is quite amazing for someone approaching eternity. It had been Angel Aimee who had single-handedly completely vanquished the Emperor Sennacherib's 185,000 strong Assyrian army when they had attacked King Hezekiah in Jerusalem. Suffice it to say, she was one tough cookie. The final and third member of the all girl Vengeance Angel Team was Angel Lily. Angel Lily was quite good with computers.

'I hear you're a Guardian Angel,' said Katie in a non-condescending way. 'That must be really tough work. I don't think I could do it.'

'Oh come off it Katie, you can do anything,' responded Jenny with a small laugh. 'I saw you on the news the other day, vanquishing that Demon those teenagers unleashed into the world.'

'Oh that,' replied a blushing Katie. 'That was mostly Aimee. They really should ban those ouija boards though.'

'Excuse me, your croissants miss,' interrupted the assistant behind the counter.

'Oh ta,' said Jenny, as she took the pastries. 'I've got to go Katie, really nice seeing you again.'

'And you! Before you go,' said Katie, fumbling in her handbag. 'Take my card. Don't hesitate to call if you need anything, or just want to meet up or something.'

Jenny took the card and left the shop. She could have talked to Katie all day, but she really did have to go, she wanted to meet Norris. Popping the card into her handbag she made a mental note to call Katie soon so they could meet up for coffee. However, the mental note got lost on its way to the *things to do department*. There were just too many tangled emotions in the way. Norris would love these chocolate covered croissant, they were heavenly. Technically, most things in Heaven were heavenly, but these croissant were particularly so. She decided to make a quick detour home to get changed before surprising Norris with breakfast. She was most definitely the best girlfriend ever. Although, she wasn't sure if she was his girlfriend yet.

Chapter 9

Norris awoke with a thump, thump and a groan, as is customary with those who have recently risen from a deep slumber by falling out of bed. The second thump was the result of Norris' semi-comatose body hitting the floor. The first thump was acoustically performed by his head contacting the side cabinet on his way towards the second thump. The groan was largely created by the first thump although the second thump also played a significant role. He rubbed his head, more out of instinct than any medical training.

There was a buzzing in his ear. It was funny because he'd expected it to be more of a ringing than a buzzing, but before he'd had a chance to fully contemplate this, the buzzing stopped. As he began to lift his rudely awakened body from the floor the buzzing came back. He stopped. The buzzing stopped. He moved. The buzzing came back. So he stopped again. The buzzing stopped again. It would have taken an averagely intelligent man a moment or two to realise that the buzzing was his front door bell, but Norris had been to university so it took him a bit longer. In fact, it wasn't until after he'd convinced himself that he'd done irreparable damage to his brain, that he realised the voice shouting 'hello' wasn't coming from his head but in fact through the letterbox. Norris put his dressing gown on and made his way downstairs. Who could be calling at this hour of the morning? He didn't know what hour it was, but his indignation certainly appeared to be suitable for someone who had just been woken up at... nine thirty-two.

Norris sleepily stumbled his way to his front door and opened it. Typical he thought, looking at the door to door salesman. He was sure he was a salesman, with his pinstriped suit, wide collared shirt with no tie, and he had knocked at his door for no apparent reason. The thing that gave it away the most though, was his broad grin. This man was definitely selling something.

'Hi,' said Death.

Before Death could even mention insurance, double-glazing, or any number of quality household cleaning products, Norris began closing the door.

'Not today thankyou.'

The door wouldn't close. A foot had somehow found itself solidly lodged in the way. A second figure, noticeably shorter, now stood next to the salesman. He recognised him, but couldn't fathom from where.

'Remember me?' Reg deliberately used the phrase, he'd even practised it. In the films, the assumed dead hero, always used this line to great effect. The recipient baddie would fall back cowering, stuttering the words - but... but you're dead. I killed you. Unfortunately, Norris hadn't learnt his lines.

'I'm sorry, but I can't quite place...' apologised Norris.

'You were in your car,' prompted Reg.

'Er, no sorry.' He didn't like to think about driving since the accident.

'Look at my face,' said a disgruntled Reg, raising his hands up defensively and twisting his face into an exaggerated expression of terror.

'But... but you're dead. I killed you,' stuttered Norris, as he faced his own personal Wessex's ghost.

At last, a bit of cowering, thought Reg, as he stepped through the doorway towards a fearful Norris (who had now stumbled back towards the stairs).

'You killed me, you pompous, middle class, idiot!' shouted Reg. 'You and your bourgeoisie Volvo estate.'

All the recent tribulations he had experienced rose to the surface and Reg did something he had never done before. He threw a punch. It hit Norris squarely on the nose.

'Ow. That hurt.'

The effect wasn't really up to the standard Reg had hoped for. Norris did not go flying back through the force of the blow. He just stood there slightly shocked, and raised his hand to his nose. Reg hit him on the nose again.

'Ow. Stop it.'

Still not the fully desired effect, but at least this time his punch made it start to bleed. Oh, he'd given someone a nose bleed; his nose was bleeding. Reg suddenly felt guilty. Norris deserved the first punch, but the second went against Reg's sense of fair play.

'Sorry,' said Reg, handing over his handkerchief.

'It's okay, I deserved it.'

'No, no you didn't. Look hit me back. Give me a nose bleed.'

'He can't,' said Death stepping inside. 'You're dead you can't bleed.'

'Really?'

'When have I ever lied to you?'

Reg let that pass. He'd never thought of it this way; he was effectively immortal. Of course, being immortal requires a certain amount of life in the first instance, and Reg was most assuredly dead. However, the fact that he was highly unlikely to die a second time, did provide him with a certain amount of immortality. It sort of followed the life after death template they promote in Sunday School, in between singing hymns about lambs and donkeys, and making Mother's Day cards out of macaroni.

As a way to test his newfound powers, Reg quickly swung a solid punch into his own nose; and promptly fell onto his backside as pain shot through his face.

'Argh,' he groaned, holding his nose. 'You said it wouldn't hurt.'

'No. I said you can't bleed,' explained Death, stepping over Reg. 'I'll get the kettle on. We've got a lot to talk about.'

'So let me get this straight,' said Norris, after the current situation had been explained to him for the umpteenth time. 'You are a ghost. Can you walk through walls?'

Reg looked up brightly.

'No, he cannot. He is effectively like you, a solid being. For a short period of time that is.'

'Oh,' said Reg and Norris in disappointed unison.

'Okay, that I can understand,' continued Norris. 'The whole Hell on strike thing, fine. But are you sure you're Death. I mean shouldn't you have a cloak and scythe?'

Death gave a deep sigh.

'So are you sure you don't want to sell me the latest innovation in carpet cleaning science?' asked Norris.

'No,' replied a thoroughly despondent Death. They should have gone with the monkey. A bunch of bananas and they would have had him on side by now.

'Okay, just one question.'

'Yes, that includes any product claiming the title super or wonder mop.'

'Er, why me?'

'Good question.' Death's gaze turned to Reg.

Norris took his lead and also looked at Reg. Reg knew he'd be in a whole lot of trouble with Death if he told the truth... he'd wanted to hit Norris. Think fast, why this man, with no apparent suitable merits for the task, other than being of an average height.

'He's got a Volvo estate.'

Both the interrogators looked bemused.

'Well, if we've got to find a suitable location for Hell on Earth. We may as well do it in comfort *and* style.'

Norris and Death had to agree, there was no arguing with that.

'Good idea,' said Death, nodding appreciatively.

Having already won the argument, Reg adopted what he considered to be one of his finer traits, and laboured the point.

'Besides, the safety record is outstanding. When you're the one travelling in the vehicle,' he quickly added, remembering his recent encounter with a Volvo estate. 'And despite its obvious support of a capitalist culture, I do believe that there would be few among the honest working proletariat, that would refute the use of this mode of transport on such a worthy quest. Furthermore...'

'Er, sorry to interrupt,' said Norris. 'I was just wondering, can I bring a friend?'

'I don't really think that's a good idea. But, if we should, you know, get a little spare time, we could visit Longleat Safari Park to feed the llamas and you could bring your friend then,' said Death in his highly polished sarcastic tone.

It was at this moment, as if in some twist of fate, that Norris' intended friend walked in through the still open door. The casual observer of recent events however, would not find any twist in the fate of this person walking through the door. They would probably argue that the very twisty nature of these events would increase the probability of this person walking through the door at this moment, and that had the person not arrived, that itself would have been more of a twist. The casual observer however, was not present to inform them of this, and therefore all three looked startled as Jenny walked in.

Reg was the first to react to her presence, standing to his feet, he gave a short bow of his head.

'M' Lady,' he said in the manner of a nineteenth century gamekeeper, although he was never quite sure why.

'Jenny. Speak of the devil.' Norris had little idea of the *faux pas* he'd just committed.

Jenny was not a Devil, she was an Angel. A fact that was not lost on Death.

'Why are you here?' he asked suspiciously.

'This is er, my friend Jenny.' Norris didn't quite feel comfortable referring to her as his girlfriend.

'If you've come for him, you can't have him,' said Jenny standing protectively in front of Norris.

'Er, do you know each other?' asked Norris peering over Jenny's shoulder.

'By reputation only. This is Death,' said Jenny.

'Oh so you are Death then, not a salesman. Wait a minute, how do you know he's Death?'

'Because...' began Death. 'It appears your *friend* just happens to be an Angel.'

'Yes, she's an angel,' confirmed Norris, looking lovingly into Jenny's eyes.

To Norris' dismay there was a look in her eyes that spoke louder than late night revellers' words; it spoke of a guilty secret.

'Sit down Norris,' she said, gently pushing him back onto the settee.

'What is it?'

'I'm so sorry, but I've deceived you.'

'You're married?'

'No, I'm an Angel.'

'A what? An Angel, what's that?'

'An Angel,' said Jenny revealing her true self.

Norris sat back, slack jawed as he watched Jenny suddenly appear before him in her full majestic brilliance, her wings spread wide, a shimmering halo of glowing light surrounding her angelic countenance.

'Oh, an Angel,' said Norris, and fainted.

People's reactions to the sudden appearance of an Angel before them varies considerably. The shepherds hid themselves and cowered, the ancient Egyptians came out in boils and sores, and Mary got pregnant. So Norris' initial reaction appeared to be quite mundane.

'That was subtle,' said Death. 'Way to break it to a guy.'

'What do you want with him?' said Jenny protectively. 'And do tell, how did he get that bloody nose?'

'I'll put the kettle on,' said Reg sheepishly disappearing into the kitchen.

'Oh good I've brought croissants,' responded Jenny, forgetting her anger for a moment.

'Excellent.'

'What's going on?' Jenny directed her question to Death.

'Well I'm sure you've read about that whole Hell going on strike thing, in the Angelic Times.'

'Yes, I'm aware of the problem,' said Jenny, although she'd read about it in the less high brow Daily Saint, which generally dealt with celebrity gossip unless something really big was happening.

'Well a team has been created to find a suitable replacement; Hell on Earth to be exact, and we are that team. Your *friend* Norris is our guide.'

'Norris, your guide. Why on Earth would you pick him?'

'He drives a Volvo estate,' said Death, with an isn't it obvious expression.

The *isn't it obvious* expression is not the easiest expression to master, particularly if you don't shrug at the same time. Death did aid his expression with a shrug on this occasion. He believed the shrug and expression necessary to avoid further questioning. He knew it didn't really make any sense at all, but a small bluff and a bit a of car talk had worked for him in the past. He'd found that women tended to accept car related excuses. Late for a date; mention car trouble, add a bit about manifolds, carburettors, and distributor caps and they soon lost interest in the conversation and any willingness to continue the argument. Tried and tested.

Jenny couldn't believe it; men and their obsession with cars. Here they all were, facing a crisis that threatened the very existence of the natural order of the universe and decisions were being made on the basis of what car someone drives. It was so typical. The Daily Saint had said that Angel Aimee from Angel Force Three had cancelled a date with a mysterious hunk to make herself 'available in this time of crisis.' But apparently she didn't drive the right type of car. Men! It was kind of exciting though, her boyfriend being the last hope of the universe. If he was her boyfriend, especially after her recent revelation. Then she remembered; Norris!

Jenny quickly turned her attention to the still comatose Norris.

'Norris. Norris,' she said gently tapping his face. 'I brought you croissants.'

It's not every day that you're told the person you recently killed by accident has caused a strike in Hell, and that you are needed to act as a guide to find a new Hell, on Earth. Furthermore, that the people that tell you this are the very person you killed and Death. Added to which your new girlfriend turns out to be an Angel who is now hitting you in the face, calling your name and waving a bag of croissants in front of you. And all this before eleven a.m. So Norris' reaction was quite understandable. He freaked out.

'I'd really like you all to leave now,' said Norris, positioning himself as far away as his settee would allow.

'I wanted to tell you, really I did. I never meant...' Jenny gulped back a tear. 'I never wanted to hurt you.'

'You lied to me.'

'I never said I wasn't an Angel.'

'You knew all along though and you never said anything. You deceived me.'

Jenny couldn't deny that. She had deceived Norris. She looked pleadingly into his eyes, but she'd hurt him and it showed.

'All I wanted was to be happy. I thought you were someone who loved me, just an ordinary girl.' Norris looked away as he spoke. 'Just someone who genuinely loved me, that's all I wanted. Ever.'

'I am ordinary.'

'You're a frigging Angel! What's ordinary about that?'

'If you knew my world, you'd know I'm nothing special. I'm just a Guardian Angel, your Guardian Angel, and I can't even do that right.'

'Look, I just want you to leave, all of you.'

'No can do I'm afraid. Because like it or not, you're our guide and we need you.' It was Death's turn to join the conversation. 'This is bigger than all of us.'

Norris looked at Death and knew he had no choice. This wasn't the salesman Death, this was a deadly serious Death, and when it comes to deadly serious no-one does it better than Death.

'Okay. But when this is over, I don't want to see any of you again.' Norris turned to Jenny. 'Any of you.'

Norris could have sworn he'd seen a tear roll down Jenny's face before she'd turned away. Maybe she was sincere. He quickly dispelled that thought. She was an Angel, what could she possibly see in him. It was probably just some joke she and her Angel friends played every now and then, pick on some mortal human sap and screw his head up.

Jenny stood up and walked into the hall, hiding her face from Norris. She didn't want him to see the tears cascading down her cheeks. She'd lost him. She was an Angel and he was a mortal, he was right, it would never work. She jumped with a start as she realised Death had followed her out.

'You know you're not actually part of the team?' said Death, in a slow deep voice. 'There's no need for you to come with us.'

'I'm his Guardian Angel. I'm going with...'

'Ah.' Death raised his hand to interrupt her. 'But, I'd like you to join us. To be honest. I think we're going to need all the help we can get on this one.'

'Really?' sniffed Jenny.

'Yes, really,' confirmed Death, handing her his handkerchief. Then dropping his voice to a low conspiratorial whisper. 'Because let's face it, they are complete imbeciles.'

Jenny gave a giggle in spite of herself.

'So you in?'

'Yes,' she said in a strong determined voice.

'Good. C'mon, we've got work to do.' Death paused before returning to the living room. 'Give him time, he'll come round. I guarantee it.'

Death hadn't truly felt any desperate need to have Jenny join them. As far as he could see, they'd just travel to a couple of sites, pick the most suitable for Hell and he could go back to life as Death again. Sure it would be handy having an Angel along for the ride but that wasn't the real reason. He wanted Jenny and Norris to work it out, to somehow overcome their differences and to be happy together. Most people would probably find it strange that Death would want to act as a match maker. Few would sign up for Death's online dating service. But few people could actually have an insight into Death's life. In his line of work he rarely got to bring lovers together. Lovers' suicide pacts rarely happened these days without one being quite a bit more reluctant than the other. His job was more about tearing loved ones away. If he was honest with himself he found this aspect of the job quite soul destroying. He never got to see partners reunited in eternal life because he was only involved in transition. He only got to see the tears of separation. Death wanted to witness love bloom for once. Plus, Jenny might have a couple of cute Angel friends and if she thought he was a nice guy, well who knows.

Simultaneously, as Death and Jenny re-entered the lounge, Reg returned with the tea. After a brief silent sipping of tea, Norris spoke up.

'I just want you all to know. I have agreed to help you and act as guide on this er, quest. And I will. But I don't believe any of you actually exist. I don't believe in any of it. There is no Heaven and Hell, no Angels, no Death and no ghosts. When you're dead that's it, final. I am an atheist. So none of you exist, ha!'

'How can you say that?' asked Reg. 'We're comrades, we're sitting here in front of you. How can you possibly believe we don't exist?'

'Because, I'm obviously insane and I've made you all up in here.' Norris tapped his head to emphasise the point. 'I'm an insane atheist.'

'Okay then, I'm glad we've cleared that up.' Death spoke with a slight sarcastic tone. 'Perhaps on that note we should start saving the Universe from disaster.'

'Hear, hear,' said Reg enthusiastically. He had been to numerous of committee meetings with the union and knew how to respond.

'Can anyone think of any suitable locations for

Hell?' asked Death.

'Perhaps we should think of places in Britain first, seeing as we're already here,' suggested Reg.

They all nodded in agreement.

'Maybe an inner city deprived area, they're supposed to be like living in Hell,' forwarded Jenny.

'Just because they're working class, sister, I don't believe that they are anymore suitable than some bourgeoisie suburbia,' countered Reg. 'Besides, I'll think you'll find that most inner city areas have now been redeveloped to cater for the needs of the middle classes at the cost of the working class.'

'I think the problem here is space,' interjected Death. 'Although this is only a temporary holding area until the dispute in Hell is resolved, we still need space and inner city areas don't have enough. There are a lot of sinners out there.'

'How about Twll Du?' said Norris jumping up excitedly.

Norris had got lost once on his way to a book festival and had called in at the Welsh town Twll Du for directions. It had ruined his holiday and this was his chance for revenge.

'Where?'

'Twll Du, it's in the Welsh valleys,' explained Norris. 'Trust me, the place is a perfect Hell.'

'Okay, let's check it out,' agreed Death. 'Twll Du here we come.'

It should be noted at this point that many of the place names referred to have been changed to protect the anonymity of the residents therein. For example, Twll Du in this instance is in fact Merthyr Tydfil.

Like so many towns and villages within this septic green isle, Twll Du was developed near a geographical site of importance. Easily defended hilltops, rivers affording fresh water, or natural seaports, often provided ideal sites for settlement.

Sometimes sites were chosen purely for their natural beauty. Twll Du was developed because of a large hole in the ground. Twll Du was a mining town.

However, since the recent decline of the mining industry, many residents have remained due to another geographical landmark; the Job Centre and Benefits Office.

Chapter 10

Gurglemouth knocked pensively on the door to Bacchaus' office. He had bad news. Giving any sort of news to Bacchaus was a risky business, but bad news, well that was tantamount to suicide. Not just your everyday suicide, but a particularly painful and long drawn out suicide involving a cheese grater.

'Enter.'

'Sire, got bad news.'

'Yes.' Bacchaus looked up from a pile of papers laid out before him on his ornate desk.

'It a travesty, dey creating a new Hell, sire.' Gurglemouth thought it best to blurt out the news quickly and get it over with.

'And you think I'm not informed of this?'

'Course not sire. I mean course you know.'

'Then why have you disturbed me?'

'Er, er. You wana cup of tea, p'haps?'

'No. Leave.'

Gurglemouth left the room with a sigh of relief. He'd got away with it. Bacchaus hadn't appeared bothered that his position in Hell was being undermined. Yet doubt crept into Gurglemouth's normally paranoid mind. This had to be bad, and when bad things happened in Hell he always bore the brunt. If Bacchaus wasn't going to do anything about it, then he would. He would be a hero, they might even build a statue in his honour, they might not flay the skin off his back to upholster furniture. Gurglemouth tightened his jaw with resolve, it was down to him. Quickly he formed a plan to stop Death and his team. He walked to his desk and made a phone call.

Demons face certain restrictions when walking the Earth amongst men, the most notable being the time restriction they incur. A Demon's presence is only permitted for a short period before they are dragged back to the Underworld, that is, all except one. When the other Demons were banished from walking the Earth, one was overlooked. His name was Iscyrus. The reason Iscyrus went unnoticed was simply that, unlike other Demons, Iscyrus looked perfectly human. Although his powers were limited as far as Demonic powers go, his ability to spend eternity walking the Earth more than compensated for his limitations.

During his countless years mingling unnoticed amongst mankind, Iscyrus had taken on many guises and jobs. He was best known as a high level politician whose Machiavellian ways caused strife and scandal. However, the fact that people didn't realise he was a Demon perhaps says more about politicians, than Iscyrus' ability to blend in. His most recent vocation was a hitman. Iscyrus truly felt he'd found his niche as a hired killer.

He carefully licked his ice cream as he walked slowly through the city park, the last bastion of green in an otherwise grey slabbed environment. The park itself was nice enough, a dog walker's paradise with numerous graffiti wearing bins. The man he was following was one such dog walker. What he had done to deserve Iscyrus' own particular brand of attention, not even Iscyrus himself knew, and he didn't care. The man stopped at his usual bench and let his dog, a red setter run free over the expanse of grass in front of the bench. Iscyrus sat next to him.

'Pleasant day,' remarked the man, more as a test to see if a *nutter* was sitting next to him, rather than a genuine conversation starter.

'Not really, well not for you anyway,' replied Iscyrus.

The man looked startled at Iscyrus' response, which was unfortunate, because it left little in the way of facial expressions for the moment when Iscyrus slid the long thin stiletto knife between his ribs and into his heart. The Demon wiped his blade on the man's trouser leg, took another lick of his ice cream, stood up and left the park.

'Pleasant day,' he said to an old couple he passed on his way through the gate.

As he approached his car, parked in a side street nearby, Iscyrus received a phone call on his business line. Driving down the street his mind wandered to his next job. This one promised to be quite interesting, an unusual and challenging target.

Chapter 11

The blue Volvo estate travelled down the A470 towards the town of Twll Du. The driver and the three passengers sat comfortably in their seats. Occupants of passing cars paid little attention to the seating arrangements contained within the Volvo. They had no idea of the pseudo political wrangling that had occurred prior to the journey, placing the people inside in their present seating arrangements. It went something like this...

'Twll Du here we come.'

Norris leant forward and picked up his keys from the table.

'Let's get this over with then.'

'I'm not getting in a car with you behind the wheel,' insisted Reg.

'Why not?'

'I've seen you drive, admittedly it was briefly, but from my angle, I wasn't impressed.'

Reg's frank declaration reminded Norris of the accident and he suddenly felt nervous about getting behind the wheel.

'Yeah, maybe you're right.'

'Come on then I'll drive,' said Death quickly grabbing the keys.

'Wait a minute.' Jenny tried to grab the keys. 'Statistically women are the safest drivers.'

'Hold on there Angel. It may surprise you, but this isn't an exercise in political correctness or women's lib. There is no way on Earth or for that matter Heaven or Hell that I'm letting a woman drive on this mission.'

'This is getting us nowhere. I suggest we take this notion to a secret ballot, and decide who's driving, democratically,' suggested Reg.

'Let Death drive.' Jenny feared the voting system ever since a humiliating defeat at the hands of Suzanne Ross, in the Head Girl elections in high school. Despite the positive exit poll results, Jenny's free cup cake and badge campaign, and the rumoured sex scandal surrounding Suzanne's own campaign, Suzanne won a landslide victory. It was the biggest margin in school history. She couldn't face that again.

'I agree,' added Norris. He didn't want the vote either, although for entirely different reasons. He couldn't be bothered.

'I vote me too. So if you'd like to join your democratically elected driver, maybe we can get underway.' Death was losing patience.

'Shotgun front seat,' shouted Norris.

Ironically, the term shotgun comes from the days of the Wild West, when the seat next to the driver was occupied by the guard who generally carried a shotgun. Despite the popularity of this position in recent times, in the Wild West it wasn't popular. The *shotgun* had to sit upfront enduring the elements, whilst others had the relative comfort of the carriage. Added to which, according to most Hollywood films, the *shotgun* usually found himself with the feathered shaft of an arrow sticking in his back before the end of the journey.

'You can't say shotgun, what about democracy?' argued Reg.

'Too late. I've said shotgun,' said Norris smugly.

'That's ridiculous. What happens if a Senator shouts to Congress, shotgun I'm President of the United States, do the others comply?' blustered Reg.

It wasn't so much travelling in the back that bothered Reg, it was more the attack on democratic procedure that shotgun represented.

'Don't know, don't think they've tried. Maybe

they do. Anyway I've got shotgun.'

Reg realised he had to try a different tactic. Democracy held little sway in school yard rules.

'Right, race you, the first to touch that lamppost down the street.' Reg sped off, without even saying go.

Norris knew he had shotgun rights to the front seat, but this was a challenge. He didn't want to look sissy. Besides he knew he could beat a slightly overweight man with short stubby legs, so he quickly sprinted after him.

Death and Jenny casually walked to the car, watching them run down the street.

'We're doomed,' sighed Death, opening the front passenger door for Jenny.

The Volvo estate caught up with Norris and Reg halfway down the street.

'Jump in,' said Death, indicating the back.

'The back,' complained both Reg and Norris in unison.

'First come, first serve.'

First come, first serve rule, always overrode *shotgun* and *race you for it*, and democracy for that matter.

And so it was that the blue Volvo estate went smoothly down the road, fellow motorists paying little attention to the seating arrangements. If they had, they may have heard something like a movie trailer in their heads. "Today, on this road, Death is behind the wheel." But they didn't, all except one. Three cars behind the Volvo, a motorist on a powerful motorbike fully clad in black leathers watched the car closely.

The biker knew all about their mission, and had his own; to disrupt theirs. He'd received a phone call earlier that day from an old patron from the Underworld. Use "extreme prejudice" and "any means necessary" the voice had instructed, and he intended to. But for now he'd have to wait until the opportunity presented itself.

In the Volvo the intrepid duo and the other two adventurous yet slightly less intrepid ones, had no idea they were being tailed. In the nature of many intrepid and even slightly less intrepid people, they were travelling West towards adventure, fame, and Twll Du. In the true spirit of Horace Greeley who had urged forward American pioneers with his words "Go West young man," the blue Volvo estate sped down the A470. Although, in this instance the only reason they were travelling West was because they started East of their intended destination. As in so many cases, the romantic ideal of heading West to adventure often follows the diktat of starting off from the East, unless you pay heed to the film *Krakatoa East of Java* when Krakatoa is actually West of Java. Although, I suppose you could always go the really long way round.

Death, Norris and Jenny didn't really consider the nuances of travelling West from East as they listened to Reg preaching about the importance of Twll Du's role in the British trade union's history.

'So in fact the Twll Du Rising of the Nineteenth century not only achieved borough status for Twll Du and ultimately the right of the vote, it also demonstrates the collective power of the working class.'

Despite Norris' holiday experience and Reg's didactic history of Twll Du, the town itself is in fact not that bad. Unfortunately, any sense of civic pride that the declaration "Twll Du is not that bad" might create, is immediately nullified by the fact that they arrived in the Twll Dyn housing estate. The Twll Dyn estate is in many ways similar to any number of crime ridden, run down, and neglected housing estates that exist throughout this green and pleasant land; only worse.

The architectural approach of the Twll Dyn

estate may be described as being of German influence. In the sense that it is very reminiscent of the German Luftwaffe's influence on London's architecture during the Second World War. The gentle green picturesque slopes of the countryside have been cunningly disguised by grey monotonous block houses. An avant-garde approach has been adopted by many of the keen gardeners in the surrounding area, making use of rusty cars, old tyres and odd bits of household furniture (worn out mattresses and fridges being the most popular) to provide a unique theme. Others merely being content with a more naturalistic style; allowing nature to reclaim their lawned and concreted areas.

The Twll Dyn residents also appear to be keen in individualising their homes. Certainly, numerous abodes have been given a customised makeover. The use of spray paint and the celebration of youth culture appears to be an ever popular design. Again, we can also see the influence of London's Blitz years with many of the houses displaying boarded up windows and crumbling brickwork. If you had to use one keyword to describe the collective effect of the residents' work it would be dilapidated. The overall effect has been to maintain house prices at a steady 1978 price range.

The arrival of the blue Volvo estate was greeted in a similar fashion to the first arrivals of Western ships to the Pacific Islands. The locals received the alien visitors with a mixture of wonder, curiosity, and suspicion. Heavily pregnant teenagers looked on admiringly at the menfolk, wondering if they would take them away to new and exotic lands, like Cardiff. The young children, at first nervously staring at the strangers, soon gained confidence and followed them (not too closely). The odd brave leader riding his bike up close enough to touch this weird vessel, encouraged by the jeers and whoops of the others. The bare chested menfolk looked on with hostility, quickly ushering the females behind them. Eventually, the tribal leader arrived in a rusty, battered old white B.M.W with blacked out windows. However, instead of trying to eat them, he tried to sell them drugs.

'Er, no really we don't need any pills,' explained Death.

The ritually tattooed leader grunted and drove off.

'I'm kind of hungry, can we get something to eat round here?' asked Norris, after the dealer had driven off.

A combination of dented pride and innate stubbornness had stopped him from accepting the croissant from Jenny earlier that morning. He regretted his decision now, but he had maintained his principles. You didn't accept a croissant from someone who had just broken your heart by revealing they were an Angel, it just wasn't the done thing.

'What about this place?' Death indicated a nearby public house. 'We can meet some of the locals at the same time.'

Norris wasn't reallysure he wanted to interact with the locals, but his stomach informed him that he had no choice in the matter.

'Yeah sure.'

Death drove into the dusty, potholed, gravel based concrete area, (that was optimistically sign posted as the car park) and they entered the Hanging Tree Inn.

The Hanging Tree Inn was named after the old oak tree standing in a lonely corner of the car park. In the past its low hung branches had provided the perfect anchor for the hangman's noose. Many a guilty man, (and the odd innocent one) had met their end under its boughs. Whilst not as renowned as its Tyburn relative, the tree had nonetheless received a degree of notoriety amongst the local population.

Even years following the demise of corporal punishment it had still commanded a healthy degree of respect. As dusk settled children would dare each other to touch the Hanging Tree, only the boldest of them accepting the challenge, as the tree was obviously haunted. Alas, as the years passed, its infamy dwindled to the distant memories of none but the oldest residents. Soon the tree's boughs became subject to makeshift swings and shelter for young lovers. Oh how the tree missed the good old days!

Death opened the door to the public house, (for the others to enter first) more out of a profound sense of impending doom and cowardice, than politeness.

The interior of the Hanging Tree Inn more than adequately achieved its role as a place you don't want to be. The aroma of the place was all stale beer and vomit. The vomit to a large degree was a result of the consumption of great quantities of the said stale beer. The once bright floral patterned seating, had long since succumbed to a dark waxy stain, that had spread throughout the pub like a persistent weed that ravages a prized garden. The dark wood panelled walls were chipped and dust clogged, with the occasional carved name of some visitor standing out in a lighter wood shade.

They quickly found a free table and sat around it. Norris deliberately sat as far away from Jenny as he could, secretly hoping she would notice. She didn't. Jenny was far too busy trying to disguise the fact that she had breasts. The thin cardigan she wore, now pulled tightly shut, did little to hide her cleavage in this male dominated arena. She felt eyes boring into her from all directions. She wanted nothing more than to sidle up closer to Norris, in a symbolic gesture that she was not available. But the morning's events hadn't gone as planned and now she wasn't even sure if she was unavailable.

Reg felt perfectly comfortable, or so he pretended to himself. These men were the hard working proletariat, they were his people. They may appear tough and hostile to the outsider, but he knew that they were comrades, and would hold honour above all else. He turned to Death.

'You're pretty tough right? I mean if you got into a fight, you'd win yeah? Being like Death and all.'

Norris also appeared to take extreme interest in Death's answer.

'I wouldn't know. I've never been in a fight. Most people I meet are already dead. They're not really interested in fighting.'

'But if you did have to fight, say, those three guys over there, looking like they want to kill us, you'd sort of kick ass right?'

Death casually looked over at the three huge muscle bound thugs standing at the bar.

'I'd like to think that if those guys started on us, I'd run away. In my line of work I've found that I meet the guys that run away a lot less than the ones who don't.'

'Oh.'

'Maybe we should order,' said Norris, changing the subject.

All four looked at the menu written in chalk on a blackboard, next to the bar. The barman sensing their intention walked over to their table. Fourteen years of working behind the bar had honed his intuition. He knew that if people looked at the menu, and hadn't eaten here before, they would probably order something to eat. His bar working skills had come at a cost however. Over the years his waist had expanded to accommodate sixteen pints, his shaved head belied his genuine baldness, and his humour had been subdued after enduring endless nights of sexist and racist rhetoric.

After giving the table a cursory wipe with a

dirty cloth, he turned to his new customers.

'Ready to order?' he asked with a broad Welsh valley accent.

'What's your soup of the day?' asked Norris indicating the board.

'That'd be home-grown baby tomato like.'

'Great, I'll have that,' replied Norris.

The other three all agreed that home-grown baby tomato soup sounded edible, and the barman disappeared into the kitchen behind the bar. It wasn't so much that they all wanted soup, it just seemed the least likely choice to kill them.

No sooner had the barman entered the kitchen, when one of the burly men standing at the bar called out to him.

'How bout some service then Gwyn?'

'Won't be a minute. Just serving these folks.'

The burly man glared at the four of them, as if the delay was their fault. Luckily the barman quickly reappeared.

'Take your time why don't you Gwyn,' grumbled the man, passing over an empty pint glass.

'I can't do everything at once you know, I'm only human after all.'

Interestingly the use of the phrase *I'm only human* can be seen to say a lot about the person using it. The barman fits into the category of people who are never really happy with their lot in life. These people have long since rejected the notion of divine creation, in favour of Darwin's theory of evolution.

They believe that over millions of years small microscopic single-celled life forms developed, and through insurmountable odds and perils, eventually crawled out of the sea. Then through further endless endeavour and life threatening trial and error finally formed into human beings. The ape descendant creatures then went on to create vast civilisations, (with poetry, art, space travel and video games). Only for one of *these* people to then say 'I'm only human.' I mean what's a small microscopic single-celled life form got to do to impress these people.

The man sighed as his drink was slowly being poured.

'I've only got one pair of hands you know,' said the barman in response.

Oh great, now they want an extra pair of hands. Makes you wonder if it was really worth leaving the sea in the first place.

It wasn't long before the barman returned to their table with a tray, on it four bowls of steaming hot greeny brown tomato soup.

'This soup is green,' stated Norris. Although it was obvious that it was green, he felt it needed mentioning.

'Yes,' confirmed the barman.

'Tomatoes are red,' stated Norris. Although again it was an obvious statement, he felt it needed mentioning.

'It's baby tomato soup.'

'When you say baby tomato you mean...' Norris struggled for the right amount of sarcasm. 'Baby as in not ripe.'

'It's baby tomato soup,' explained the barman. 'Baby as in green.'

Norris' sarcasm was wasted on the barman. That is one of the reasons that sarcasm often plays second fiddle to anger when complaining. Sarcasm requires a certain amount of intelligence from the recipient to truly have an effect, whereas anger only requires a lot of shouting.

Although Norris' sarcasm had little affect on the barman, it did receive an understanding ear from the three men standing at the bar. Unfortunately, they had their own reason why sarcasm should play second fiddle to anger. Anger was profoundly more fun, as more often than not, it involved hitting people.

'You taking the piss?' enquired one of them. 'Coming 'ere thinking you're better than us.'

Two of the thugs walked over, leaving the third burly man standing at the bar. They obviously believed that two of them would be enough to deal with the outsiders. The one in the lead had thick dark black eyebrows and a face that looked somehow squashed flat, his companion sported a long scar down the one side of his face. Reg decided to intervene. These were the sort of people he understood; the good honest proletariat. He stood up blocking their path to Norris.

'Brothers, we're comrades in our struggle against the bourgeoisie. I myself wore a button badge supporting the miner's strike of the eighties.'

The punch hit Reg squarely on the chin.

At times of danger and violence the body often takes over from the brain. While the brain is considering its options and the correct procedure for such an occurrence, the body reacts. Natural instincts take over. Reg's body took over in this instance. While his brain was still floundering around with the question 'why did that happen?' his body had already understood, evaluated, and devised the correct reaction. It decided the correct procedure was to fall over... so it did.

After punching Reg, the flat faced man decided to emphasise his point to Norris. As he strode forwards, Jenny stepped in his way. This was an unusual occurrence and gave the thug a bit of a dilemma. In a fight people usually moved out of his way; quickly. They did not deliberately block his path, added to which, it was a woman standing in his way. You never hit a woman. Unless you're drunk. It's okay then, because you're drunk. He prided himself on the fact that he'd never hit a woman without drinking at least four pints first. After all, he did have morals. As the flat faced man hesitated, (considering whether two pints was drunk enough to hit a woman) Jenny acted.

'Lord forgive me for what I am about to do.'

It took half a second for the impact of Jenny's foot with his groin to reach full potential. Dilemma solved. The thug crumpled to the floor; his morals intact. Angels are extremely good at supporting moral conviction.

With the first attacker successfully vanquished, the Angel turned her attention to the second. The burly man at the bar, seeing her back turned, charged over. Norris leapt from his chair onto the man's back in a desperate attempt to stop him. Unfortunately, the man had generated too much momentum and Norris was left clinging to his back as he crashed into Jenny. The burly thug wrapped his arm around the Angel's neck. With a swift twist she grabbed his arm and ducked low. The attacker was flung over her shoulder in a somersault, landing on his back with a muffled crash, (the muffled effect caused by Norris still clinging desperately to the assailant's back as he landed). Although the majority of his fall was broken by Norris, the man's shoulder had dislocated leaving him rolling on the floor in agony. As Norris lay winded from the fall, his eye caught Death ducking down beneath the table.

'Dropped my spoon,' explained Death, holding up the said spoon as evidence.

Forgetting the remaining attacker, Jenny bent down next to Norris.

'Are you okay?'

Norris wanted to say I'm fine, thanks for your concern, but watch out that guy behind you is about to hit you with a chair. Instead, he just gasped for air and hoped she understood.

The scarred bar room brawler had indeed picked up a chair. He was an advocate of the superpowers policy during the eighties: The more destructive the weapon you have the better. This ideology led to the nuclear arms race and an unprecedented escalation of weaponry. Like a charging lion, they wanted the biggest claws. Yet sometimes the simplest and smallest attacks are overlooked. The lion's claws are little use against the mosquito's bite. The nuclear bomb is useless against a fanatic terrorist with a backpack full of explosive, and a heavy chair raised above your head is nullified by a hard kick in the shin from Reg.

The man dropped the chair as pain struck his lower leg.

'Ah ha!' yelled Death jumping up next to him, holding his spoon up as a weapon.

The blow to his shin left the final aggressor hopping, his head lowered and his hands covering his wounded leg. Death took his opportunity. With a downward swing he brought the rounded disk like end of the spoon hard upon the man's exposed head. Still hopping the thug raised his hands to the crown of his head.

'Ow!'

Reg still in a prone position, let loose another kick, this time aimed at the other shin. The scarred man lowered his hands to his newly attacked shin, leaving his head exposed again. Death struck.

'Ow!'

Reg and Death's attacks became almost rhythmic. Each taking alternate turns to strike their opponent. Eventually between hops and *ows* their beleaguered victim backed away, hands raised.

'Okay. Okay enough. You win.'

Death and Reg ceased their attack and the remaining local thug cowered off to a nearby corner to nurse his wounds.

'This may be a good time to leave,' suggested Norris, finally getting his breath back.

'Yeah, I think you're right,' said Death nodding.

Death and Reg casually picked up Norris and made their way to the door. Jenny followed behind.

'Thank you,' said Jenny to the top of the barman's head, which was just protruding over the top of the bar.

There was a muffled reply. 'You're welcome.'

Stepping outside the Hanging Tree Inn, the four companions took a moment to regain their bearings. Anyone who has spent an afternoon in a drinking establishment will understand this, as the outside world appears to reside in a different reality to the one you just left; a starkly brighter reality.

Across from the entrance a young teenage boy sat side saddle on a bicycle, casually spinning the pedal with his foot.

'Wanna buy some alloys, mate?' he asked.

'No thanks,' said Norris.

'Only fifty quid.'

'No you're alright.'

'Okay, your loss.'

It didn't take them long to discover that the boy was in fact correct. It was their loss. The Volvo sat forlornly in the car park, its wheels replaced by four piles of precariously stacked bricks. The boy cycled up behind them.

'You sure you don't wana buy some alloys?'

'Why you little sh...' said Norris, physically restrained by Reg.

'Okay,' conceded Death, opening his wallet. 'Fifty quid right.'

'Nah hundred quid.'

'You just said fifty quid,' complained Death.

'Supply and demand init.'

'Fine, just give us the wheels.'

The boy gave a whistle and a group of young entrepreneurs arrived pushing Norris' wheels along the ground.

'Nice doing business with you,' said the boy riding off, counting his money.

'Aren't you going to fit them?' asked a dejected Norris.

The boy laughing, shouted back. 'We're not bloody quick fit garage you know.'

'Well hope to see you again, soon.' Death enjoyed his concealed threats.

All four looked despairingly at the wheels dumped next to the car.

'I think I should take this opportunity to make notes on the suitability of each location we visit.' Reg produced a small black notebook. 'Seeing as I'm the most qualified for such an undertaking, I do feel the need for a vote is, although valid, nevertheless unnecessary. Any objections?'

Reg's belief that he was the most qualified largely revolved around the fact that he had a little black notebook. He imagined it would be the sort of book that Lenin would have carried around with him. He found it invaluable when noting down substandard working conditions, composing small political speeches to address his fellow workers with, and for writing shopping lists. It also had a small pencil concealed within its binding which was rather nifty.

'I suppose that means you're not going to help with the wheels?' inquired Norris, with a slight edge to his voice.

'As much as I believe in the honesty of manual endeavour, I fear that the importance of a concise report has greater importance on this occasion.'

Norris sighed and directed himself towards Death.

'Come on then let's get on with it.'

'I've got one thing to say to you.' Death pointed inwardly to his suit. 'Armani.'

'I'll help,' said Jenny enthusiastically.

'I can manage.'

'Come on it'll be fun.'

'Okay,' conceded Norris. 'Pass me those nuts,

er, I mean wheel nuts.' He wasn't too sure if you were allowed to say *nuts* to an Angel.

In spite of his gripe over fitting the wheels without the aid of Death and Reg, Norris had to admit he was enjoying himself. This was singularly due the closeness of Jenny during the work. Every time their hands met with the passing of a wheel nut or the tyre wrench, his heart leapt. On two occasions his upper arm had brushed against her body. Why did she have to be an Angel? She was obviously toying with him wasn't she? Still he had to admit, despite the lies and deceit, he still kind of liked her.

Jenny was also enjoying herself immensely. She'd once read an article on changing a car wheel and now she was doing it for real. She always had a great time with Norris, they always found such fun stuff to do.

As Norris and Jenny finished tightening the last nut, Reg recapped his notes to them.

'Okay. Plus points. A sufficient bus and train service. Much of the housing is of a standard suitable for Hell. Plenty of available land for expansion. However, I, we...' Reg gave a nod towards Death. 'Do feel that an even greater expanse of land is needed, what with the amount of sinners that modern society is creating. Another minus point, and this one's a biggy. It's not exactly hot. Hell, well, Hell is hot. On the whole, a good start though, but I think we should maybe try out somewhere warmer. I... we, give Twll Du a Hell rating of seven out of ten.'

Reg waited for applause. It didn't come.

'Any suggestions where next?' asked Death.

'I hear Australia's pretty hot,' voiced Norris. 'And they've got a lot of ferocious things that try to eat you.'

'It used to be a British penal colony so it must be pretty bad,' added Reg. 'They often sent the honest workers who toiled on the land out there. Just for stealing a loaf of bread to help feed their families, because they were only paid a pittance by the bourgeoisie landowners.'

Death cut off Reg before his tirade continued. 'Australia it is.'

Dostoevsky once claimed: "The degree of civilisation in a society can be judged by entering its prisons." It should be noted that many people believe that prisoners have *too easy* a time in prison *nowadays*. However, if they think they have it too easy nowadays, they should look back into our history. Criminals got sent to Australia. These days we go there on holiday. I mean, how easy can you have it? It's hard to imagine that in few years time people will want to take their holidays in Wandsworth Prison. Interestingly, Dostoevsky is currently residing in the second level of Hell. His sentence is under appeal as it is believed that he was framed by a Nihilist. He has been recently quoted as saying "the afterlife isn't very civilised at all."

'So how are we going to get to Australia?' asked Norris.

'Drive,' remarked Death casually.

'We can't exactly drive all the way to Australia,' said Norris wiping the oil from his hands with a rag. 'It kind of involves flying, and anyway it would take forever even if we could drive.'

'Nah, we'll drive.'

Even with his recent, slightly unhinged approach to reality, Norris still fully understood the basic concepts of travel.

'And how do you propose we'll drive all the way to Australia?'

'By stopping.'

'How do you get to the other side of the world by stopping?'

'By stopping really quickly.'

'Getting to Australia by stopping. Doesn't make sense,' said Norris. 'No matter how quickly you do it.'

Death felt like saying painting yourself green and sleeping in a tree house doesn't make sense either, but he thought better of it. Better just to explain it now and move on, rather than go through this every time they needed to make a Pan Dimensional Jump.

'Look it's simple,' Death declared, although he knew it wasn't. 'You're aware the world is spinning right?'

'Yeah.'

'Absolutely,' agreed Reg.

'Well all we have to do is point in the right direction. And stop. Really quickly. By the time we start again we'll have travelled miles. The world will have carried on underneath us, see?' explained Death. He left out the bit about cross-dimensional plane theory deliberately, as this often confused mortals. 'Okay, shall we make a move? Now does anyone know the way to Australia?'

'Er, down?' Reg wasn't really sure, but *down* did seem like a reasonable estimation.

'I'll ask,' Death headed towards a previously unnoticed drunk tramp propped up against a low crumbling wall skirting the car park.

Norris gave a startled jump. He hadn't noticed him before. This is hardly surprising, as homeless drunks appear to have an innate ability to blend in and disappear into their surroundings, such as a urine smelling doorway. However, this is not the case. Your typical doorway dwelling drunkard has no such camouflaging capability. They are not inner city chameleons. It has more to do with your average person's capacity to subconsciously ignore such people. Borne no doubt through a fear of having to explain why they don't have any spare change; an ability that is nurtured from an early age. A child who asks why that strange man is sleeping on the park bench and can I pat his doggy, is quickly ushered away by their instructive parent. After all, it is easier to point out the cute baby ducklings in the pond, than to explain how social inadequacies and a failure of the system led to that man being there. Besides I don't have any spare change.

Jenny had noticed the drunk and had already made a mental note to make some inquires. Some Guardian Angel was definitely not fulfilling their responsibilities. Reg, his attention now draw to the drunk, felt like telling him not to worry and that come the revolution everyone will be given an equal opportunity, and that a social structure would be put in place to help people in his situation. He didn't. Mainly because he didn't want to *butt in,* but also because he didn't have any spare change.

The drunk looked up at Death with bleary eyes. 'Yessh?'

'Can you tell me the way to Australia?'

'It'sh sthat way.' The drunk waved his hand in the general direction of a nearby concrete lamppost and a urinating mongrel dog. Although having no discernible camouflage skills, winos are superb at giving directions; it's just no-one ever asks.

'Can I ashk you queshion?'

'Go ahead.'

'Whatsh sh'it ev'rytshing 'bout, you sh' know?'

'Forty-two.'

The drunk wobbled up to his feet smiling. 'Thanksh.' He shook Death's hand and wandered happily off.

'Everybody in the car,' ordered Death, ushering them into the Volvo.

As soon as the car was fully loaded with its passengers Death accelerated rapidly towards the slightly damp lamppost, and Australia. At the last second before impact he slammed down on the brakes (really quickly). The only person to witness how quickly Death stopped was a leather clad biker. The car blurred and disappeared from his vision. This is going to be a challenge he thought to himself.

Chapter 12

Nothing can quite prepare someone for a pan dimensional jump between planes of existence. No matter how many episodes of Star Trek you watch, or how many times you read *Pan Dimensional Jumping for Complete Beginners,* you cannot truly envision how overwhelmingly dull it actually is. The crux of the problem lies with the fact that it involves stopping. The actual jump takes place when you're stopped, which is tantamount to doing nothing. Even staunch Buddhists agree that doing nothing is in fact quite boring and doing nothing very quickly is no better. A suggestion was made that the introduction of a spectrum of lights whizzing past may make it slightly more enjoyable. However, this was not deemed very cost effective and rather pointless as the journey was over so quickly.

Reg was disappointed. 'Is that it? We've travelled thousands of miles in a nano second and that's it? No whizzing lights, nothing?'

'What did you expect?' asked Death.

'I don't know. But that was really boring.' Reg's observations were particularly acute considering he'd never even read *Pan Dimensional Jumping for Complete Beginners.*

Reg and the rest immediately realised that they were no longer in Twll Du, or even Britain, because of the not so fatal mistake they had made. A not so fatal mistake is very similar to a fatal mistake, the only really stand out difference being the lack of fatalities. The mistake in this instance, is in many ways identical to the mistake made by thousands of British holiday makers each year. It is based on the ridiculous presumption that the attire you leave one country in will be suitable for the one you are travelling to. For example, go to Heathrow Airport when the next flight from Malaga is due, or another suitably hot country, and witness the shivering passengers disembark in shorts and vest tops to be greeted by rain and extremely mild temperatures. The reverse is often equally true, and in this particular case the reverse was true.

'Wow, it's hot!' complained Reg, loosening his tie. 'I mean really hot.'

'Is it?' queried Death. For some reason he never felt the heat, he was always cold. Not stone cold just a nice level of chill.

'Maybe we should wind down the windows,' suggested Jenny cheerfully.

As they wound down the windows they realised their second not so fatal mistake. Perhaps the most welcoming of Australian residents instantly turned up *en masse* to greet them. Hundreds of flies instantly began buzzing excitedly around the occupants of the car. Even the Australian Tourist Board's carefully scripted *g'day mates* and broad smiles fall short when compared to the genuine enthusiasm displayed by the average Australian fly upon meeting a visiting holiday maker.

'Drive,' requested Norris in an Hitleresque fashion. 'Get us out of here.'

He hated flies. So much so that he was willing to put up with spiders for it. He detested the thought of how flies eat their food. Similar to bulimic super models they eat, then regurgitate it. However, only flies eat the regurgitated food, bulimic super models are too conscious of the calories to do that.

The car sped away along the deserted road leaving a trail of red dust and coughing and spluttering flies.

Interestingly, sixty seven percent of the flies they left behind had the less dominant red eye gene. If you don't find this interesting then you're obviously not a genetic scientist or my third year biology teacher.

Without any discernible map reading skills, or in fact a map to prove this lack of skill, the occupants of the Volvo had little choice but to follow the road and hope to end up somewhere.

'Actually I've rarely encountered a road that leads to nowhere,' replied Death to his passengers' concerned enquiries. 'Even the ones that don't lead anywhere come from somewhere so at the very least we've got a fifty fifty chance.'

As luck would have it, the road did lead somewhere. Although that somewhere was as close to nowhere as you could possibly get without actually going there. That somewhere was called Dunnygong Springs.

Dunnygong Springs is described in the 1972 edition of the *Western Australian Tourist Board's Guide* as a "traditional slice of outback Australia." It continues to state that "if you should be in the vicinity then it's probably worth the visit." Dunnygong Springs never got a mention in any of the subsequent editions of the guide. This was largely due to three important reasons. Firstly, a prominent dignitary famously parodied the guide saying "...if you should be in the vicinity then it's probably not worth the visit." Secondly, the writers responsible for compiling the W.A.T.B Guide have consecutively since 1972 failed to find Dunnygong Springs on their travels. Finally, and possibly in defence of the guide, the town hasn't changed in any notable way to actually warrant an updated version anyway.

The dusty road that led directly into (and much more usefully directly out of) Dunnygong Springs, stopped abruptly outside the town's entertainment epicentre; Walt's Hotel and Bar. Death pulled up next to a couple of severely dented pickup trucks, and a bored looking water buffalo. The buffalo looked up at the new arrivals once, then continued being bored.

'Told you the road would lead somewhere,' stated Death.

'Are you sure?' quipped Norris. 'I mean there's not much here is there?'

'Well as a technicality, it's probably better not to have too many people living here,' suggested Reg. 'I would imagine people would get quite uptight about living next to Hell. House prices would drop for a start and that's never a good thing for the working man.'

The town was indeed sparsely populated. In fact it only really consisted of five businesses. Next to Walt's Hotel and Bar stood the Dunnygong Spring's combined Post Office, Convenience Store and Pharmacy. Next to that Jessops Hardware and Supplies. Then on the other side of town, situated fifty yards away, was the obligatory large corporate American fast food diner, and finally Boots and Bags Fashion Boutique. Boots and Bags was by far the least successful of the town's business sector, so much so, that nobody, to anyone's recollection, had actually bought anything from there. The fact that in spite of this, the shop had remained open for twenty years, led to many of the locals believing that it was actually a front for selling drugs. Unfortunately for the proprietor, Boots and Bags Fashion Boutique had failed to sell any drugs either. The only reason that it had not faced foreclosure for so long was that the bank had been unable to locate it in order to serve notice.

'Let's go inside,' suggested Norris. 'Maybe we can get a map.'

Contrary to the usual reaction to the appearance of Jenny in any male dominated area, the men in Walt's paid her little attention. The majority sat in the far corner, huddled around a small portable television placed on a bar stool. They gave a quick glance across at the newcomers then continued with their activities. The fact that they paid no attention to Jenny had little to do with the importance of what they were doing. It had been so long since most of the men in Dunnygong Springs had seen an attractive female they had forgotten what one looked like, and therefore, had failed to recognise one when one had actually appeared.

The eponymous owner of Walt's stood behind a short stubby squared off bar in the corner. Its rustic pine delicately contrasted with the pale blue and orange wood panelled walls, a contrast that would make any passing interior designer blanch in terror.

'Well what'll it be mates?' Walt brushed the remainder of his hair across the long since bald top, in an attempted display of youth and vigour. Walt had been a long time subscriber of *Bonza Jugs*. He recognised an attractive female when he saw one.

'We were wondering if we could buy a map?' asked Death. 'Of the area.'

'Sure thing mucker, five dollars.'

'Do we have any Australian money?' whispered Reg in Death's ear, or at least as close to it as he could get with the height difference.

'Yeah, I've got every major currency. You never know where you'll end up in my line of work.'

Death handed over the five dollars which quickly disappeared into the cash register. Walt bent down below the bar and pulled out a blank piece of paper which he proceeded to draw on with a pencil almost worn beyond use.

'There you go mate,' Walt passed the completed *map* to Death.

It wasn't so much the fact that he'd paid for a hand drawn map that bothered Death. It was the more simplicity of it that bothered him. The *map* consisted of five buildings, (granted they were neatly labelled) and a line, which he presumed was the road. Nevertheless, he was determined not to show that he was bothered by the con.

'This line, it's that road right?'

'Only mucking with ya fella. Here's your wonga back,' laughed Walt, passing Death the five dollars back. 'But that'll be the closest you'll get to a map around here. Coz there's little to map. One road in, one road out.'

'What about all this land here?' asked Death pointing to the blank area around the pencil lines.

'Well there's nothing there really, mostly bush.'

'Does anybody own it?'

'Well that old goat McKinley lays claim to most of it. But he's in dispute with the Aboriginal peoples over it.' Walt leant forward and put his elbow on the bar. 'You see, the Aborigines believe that we belong to the land, so we can't own the land. Take those mountains over yonder, they'll be there long after you and I are gone, so how can we own them? It's like two fleas arguing over who owns the dingo. So the Aborigines are trying to get ownership of their land back so they can say nobody owns it.'

At that moment the gathered patrons crowding around the television erupted with angry shouts and enthusiastic gesticulation of the offensive kind. One voice could be heard distinctly over the general commotion.

'Ya eye-gouging dirty kiwi b'stard.'

Reg recognised the vernacular of the good honest workers and decided to make his acquaintance with them.

'Who's playing?' he asked the nearest supporter.

'Aussie verses those stinking Kiwis,' a dusty tanned man replied.

'Ahh, rugby.' responded Reg knowingly.

'Nah mate it's the ladies netball.'

'But that ones got a beard!'

'Right you are there. I wouldn't want any sexual

relations with her, if you take my meaning. But I gotta admit, she's the finest goal attack this game has ever seen.'

As if to prove his point, the bearded goal attack slotted the ball neatly in the netted hoop. The gathered support erupted again, this time with glee.

'She really is good. What's her name?' asked Reg, when the commotion had finally died down.

'Frank Bellows.'

'Frank?'

'Yep. Apparently, her folks didn't realise she was a girl until she was thirteen either.'

Meanwhile, in a minor sub plot Elle Bradley sat at her desk. Those who knew Elle always found it hard to believe how she could have risen to her position, considering all the hardship she'd endured throughout her life. Elle had been born as a twin to a poor family. Her parents had always tried to provide for Elle and her twin sister Beatrice as best as they could. Sadly, one Christmas, tensions rose when young Elle didn't get the present she really wanted and a terrible argument broke out between her and her parents. The outside observer would see it as a cruel twist of fate that the house would burn down that very night with her parents trapped inside.

From that moment on Elle's life took on a series of misfortunes. With no relatives able to take care of the twin eight year olds, Elle and Beatrice were sent to Mary Immaculate Orphanage PLC. For some inexplicable reason, Beatrice was always more popular with all the nuns who ran the orphanage. Sister Janet, who died falling down two flights of stairs, preferred Beatrice. As did Sister Margaret who fell to her death from the third floor balcony. Little Sister Charlotte always saved extra sweets for Beatrice, before her gardening accident with a hedge trimmer. The list went on. Of the twenty or so replacement nuns who came and died at the orphanage, not one preferred poor Elle.

Eventually the day came for the twins to leave the orphanage. Some people would consider it extremely lucky that the twins left when they did, as less than two hours later a gas explosion destroyed the orphanage and killed the majority of the occupants. So it was that the twins entered the outside world.

The trend continued outside the orphanage, with Beatrice being the most popular of the two, particularly with the boys. Despite being very similar in looks, and Elle's willingness, Beatrice always seemed to get her man while poor Elle was left on the sidelines. Ronald, who was killed in a hit and run incident, preferred Beatrice. James, Beatrice's longest boyfriend, who died when he fell off a ladder, had actually rejected Elle's advances in favour of her sister. Pete Dovey had even asked Beatrice to marry him before he went missing on a fishing trip. As always, Elle was there for Beatrice when misfortune struck, assuring her that it wasn't her fault that the people close to her always seemed to die tragically.

Perhaps the greatest upheaval in Elle's life came when both sisters were shortlisted for a job they both wanted. Naturally, Beatrice got the job and then inexplicably, committed suicide a few hours after receiving the news. The not entirely convincing suicide note proclaimed that Beatrice could not bear to have "stolen" the job that was "far more suited to the talents of Elle." In honour of her dead sister's wishes Elle took the job the next day, despite the obviously traumatic time she was experiencing. The local police inspector even had the audacity to suspect Elle. This was due to a number of factors. Firstly, the suicide note was written on a computer and was evidently written after Beatrice was pronounced dead. Secondly,

Beatrice appeared to have been very keen to get the job in her interview. But most of all, because of her method of suicide. Beatrice had committed suicide by stabbing herself in the back with a large pair of scissors, eight times. The case was eventually thrown out of court, as although there were serious doubts over suicide as a verdict, the stabbing motion was committed by a right handed person. In an amazing piece of courtroom dramatics Elle caught an apple thrown by her lawyer with her left hand! Case dismissed.

Elle's rise in the company was without precedent. As secretary to the C.E.O, she was as surprised as everyone else when he decided to leave and live as a hermit 'somewhere as far away from here as possible.' She appeared to be even more stunned when he also left the day to day running of the company to his secretary, who was now to be considered the C.E.O. In less than six months she had risen from secretary to C.E.O in one of the world's most prominent investment companies. Yes, those who knew Elle always found it hard to believe how she could have risen to her position, considering all the hardship she had endured throughout her life. Those who knew Elle really well, knew she was an evil bitch.

Elle Bradley sat at her desk. Her work kept her extremely busy, typing with her one hand and scribbling notes and answering the phone with the other. Nevertheless, she still found time in her overworked brain to muse how handy it was to be ambidextrous. Completely ignoring her workload, Elle immediately stopped everything, as he phone rang. Not her everyday business phone; the other one. Elle knew better than to let it ring more than once. She picked up the innocuous looking phone on the far end of the desk.

'Hello,' she answered nervously.

During the fifteen minute conversation that

followed Elle's face slowly brightened. No sooner had she hung up than she bellowed for her personal assistant.

'Wilson! Get in here.'

Wilson entered before the sentence was finished.

Miss Bradley?'

Elle hated the way that woman somehow put emphasis on the word *miss*. It was as if she was commenting on Elle's inability to find love. She sensed she was really saying most women are married at your age, just look at me, I'm more successful than you because I have a husband. But good help was hard to find and Susan Wilson was good.

'I need Mr Becker in here immediately. We're pulling all our available assets into the land appropriation market.'

'Are you sure? The climate isn't particularly good for land purchase at the moment.'

Wilson was good, she knew her stuff, but she didn't know what Elle knew. She had insider information.

'Oh yes, I'm sure.'

Wilson scurried out in search of Mr Becker. Miss Bradley leant back in her chair. Long ago she'd sold her soul to the Head of the Underworld, but she'd been clever. She hadn't sold it all at once, each favour had cost her a percentage. Each time she'd called upon *his* assistance she'd neared her status of lost soul. She was very near now, but this information was worth it. With this information she could make enough money to retire to a multimillionaire's lifestyle. She would never have to call on *his* favours again.

'Come on, we're going.' Death put his hand on Reg's shoulder.

This action would probably send shivers of fear down the spine of any other man, but not Reg. Not because he was braver than any other man, but because he figured Death and him were mates. In the short time they'd known each other they'd been through a lot and besides, Reg quite liked Death.

Reg turned around to see Norris bolting out the door of Walts'. He didn't even get the chance to call shotgun before Norris had claimed the front passenger seat. Damn his new found obsession with the gritty sport of women's netball, it had cost him the front seat, he thought, as he climbed into the back seat behind Death.

'Where we off muckers?' asked Reg, in a slightly Australian vernacular.

He'd always been susceptible to picking up regional dialects and accents. Someone once told him it was a sign of a friendly person. Apparently, you imitate other dialects in order to fit in and make friends. Reg didn't really believe this, he figured it was because his own accent and dialect was so dull.

'We're gonna check out the McKinley place,' replied Norris, rather smugly from his front seat position. 'Open the window would you.'

As Reg leant forward to wind the rear window down, it suddenly shattered. A short whizzing sound followed and the opposite window also shattered.

'What you doing? No need to smash it!'

'I didn't. I think someone just shot at us.'

Two hundred metres away the leather clad biker cursed as his first shot went awry. He pulled back the bolt action of the rifle and another bullet clicked into the chamber.

'Are you sure someone's shooting at us?' Death casually enquired. 'It's just I've usually got this kind of spooky sixth sense about the whole shooting and killing business.'

'I'm quite sure,' gulped Reg, as a second bullet exploded the rear windscreen.

'Get us out of here!' screamed Norris.

'Okay, chill out.' Death turned on the ignition.

'I'm the mortal one remember, you lot haven't got anything to worry about.'

'That's not strictly true. See Jenny, although immortal, has a mortal life on Earth, if she dies here she's banished to the afterlife. Same thing happens with Demons.' Death pushed the car into gear. 'And Reggie boy feels pain, remember when he hit himself on the nose. So getting shot is not a nice experience for him either. And this suit is Armani. Can you imagine my distress if I got blood on it? So, you're not the only one with something at stake here.'

Death sped off, sending a cloud of red dust in the car's wake. A third bullet ricocheted off the boot of the car and relieved the boredom of the water buffalo, who now wondered why someone had shot his tail off.

'Make a jump. That pan dimension thing!' yelled a non-pacified Norris.

Death stopped the car.

The leather clad assassin watched as the car disappeared. He'd missed his chance, this time at least. He knew his friend would send him where he needed to go, and next time he'd get the job done. As he stood up he noticed someone standing next to him. The someone smiled serenely. Strange, he thought, not many people would smile serenely when faced with a gun toting assassin. Even fewer could get this close to said gun toting assassin without him noticing. In fact, even less than that, only one. The one that is only known in certain inner circles. The one whose name is spread only through legend. The leather clad hitman whispered the name, the last word of his mortal life.

'Iscyrus.'

Chapter 13

Bacchaus hung up the phone in his office and leant back in his plush chair.

'Gurglemouth come here would you my dear fellow?' His tone was sickly smooth.

As Gurglemouth entered from the adjacent room he felt nervous. Gurglemouth always felt nervous when entering his master's private office, but this time he felt it particularly so. Bacchaus was a bad 'un and never used a friendly tone when calling for him.

'Stand there and stretch your arms out, either side that's a good fellow,' Bacchaus continued amicably.

Instantly, with their customary puff of smoke, two imps appeared carrying tape measures and began taking Gurglemouth's measurements. For a short ill perceived moment Gurglemouth believed he was being measured for a suit. Then slowly out of a shadowy corner stepped Georgio Dupont, Bacchaus' personal interior designer. Georgio began pinching at Gurglemouth's sweating skin.

'Ah, such a magnificent stretchy quality, no. And the colour, so rich, so vibrant. It is something that only an artist such as myself can truly appreciate.'

Regardless of his fears, Gurglemouth felt quite flattered. Then the reality struck him.

'No master, why?' he whimpered.

'Ah yes why?' Bacchaus' tone had changed, the anger seeped through his words. 'You interfered with my plans. That amateur assassin you sent came so close to disrupting months of careful meticulous work.'

'But master, sir I... I thought dat I help you. I... I

thought dey undermine your greatness. Take Hell off you.'

'You thought! You thought that I, Bacchaus, could be undermined by such a thing! You thought that I, in my infinite wisdom would allow my power to be stripped from me. You thought that such a weak and feeble mind as your's could possibly be of assistance to me!' Bacchaus paused for a moment, resting his two index fingers to his upper lip. 'Of course, you were only displaying loyalty, as misguided as it may be.'

'Yes... yes master. Gurglemouth serve you.'

'And I would have to be some kind of demonic monster to punish you for that. Oh wait, I am. Georgio, make me a footstool.'

The soft shimmering hue of the vast sandy desert expanse stretched out before the small mammal. It may have been a meerkat, but to be honest I'm not quite sure; the natural world has never been my strong point. With a sudden flick of its tail it bounded over the steep side of a particularly large dune. Its rapid exit caused by the explosive eruption of sand thrown into the air as the Volvo estate slammed into the dune's side. The occupants sat still as the settling sand pattered against the tin bodywork.

'Where are we?' Norris turned to Death.

'I'm not exactly sure. I didn't really have time to contemplate the direction, distance, or the time we spent stopped. But I'm pretty sure we're not where we were. And we're not in the ocean, which is usually a good thing.'

'Could that happen?' asked Reg from the rear seat.

'Of course. But I figured it was a justifiable risk. Someone was shooting at us.'

'Are you sure they were shooting at us?' Jenny, being an Angel, always tried to look at the positive side of mankind. 'I mean, maybe they mistook us for something else.'

Death glanced dubiously at her. 'What like a couple of rabbits?'

'Well maybe.'

'A couple of rabbits driving a big blue estate car?'

'Well whoever it was is long gone now.' Norris wanted to stick up for Jenny but couldn't quite bring himself to entirely back her up. So he opted for the *change the conversation* tactic instead. 'So any ideas how we can find out where we are?'

The change the conversation tactic is a technique used by politicians throughout the ages. For example, when Himmler questioned Hitler about his relationship with his niece. 'Why don't we invade Poland.' Or when Goering questioned Hitler about wearing ladies underwear. 'Why don't we invade Russia.' Or when Eva Braun asked Hitler to marry her. No wait, he just shot himself that time.

'Nope, haven't a clue. Although the amount of sand sort of indicates we're in a desert. Or a very large egg timer. But I'm inclined to go with desert.' Death answered dryly.

'So you really have no idea whatsoever where we are?'

'Listen, pan-dimensional jumping isn't like dusting crops kid.' Death was a big *Star Wars* fan and enjoyed using the line. Okay, granted the line didn't exactly fit, Norris wasn't the farm boy type of character and pan-dimensional jumping was an entirely different mode of transport to doing a light speed jump, but what the heck it made him sound like Han Solo. 'But, I should be able to use the stars to establish our position once it gets dark, like the ancient mariners and all that.' Death casually waved his hand towards the sky.

'You can do that? That's really cool.' Norris was impressed.

The others nodded their agreement.

'Er. Yer of course.' This wasn't exactly true. Death justified his little lie by the fact that he knew which constellation *The Plough* was, and by the fact that they had a more pressing problem. 'Problem is the car appears to be somewhat knackered.'

'What do you mean? What's wrong with it?' Norris was upset. It was his car after all. The distinct possibility that this could mean his ultimate death in the savage wilderness had yet to occur to him. 'Hey, wait a minute. I could die out here!' He figured it out.

'Okay, calm down. Firstly, I mean it won't start. Secondly, I don't know. I'm not a mechanic. But when I turn the key nothing happens and I know enough to know that means the car is knackered. And finally, yes probably.'

'I'm going to die?'

'You're not going to die.' Jenny shot Death a dirty look, it wasn't particularly dirty (she was an Angel after all) but it was nevertheless enough to indicate that he had been a touch heartless in his last statement.

'I am. I'm gonna die out here, wherever here is.' Norris turned to face Reg. 'This is your fault, you wanted this. It's revenge for me killing you that's what this is!'

'I didn't plan this. Anyway, I had my revenge when I hit you on the nose.'

'But you got me into this.'

'And you got me into this first. Maybe if you had learnt to drive properly.'

'Okay enough!' Jenny used her matriarchal voice. 'This bickering is getting us nowhere. Why don't we stop arguing about whose fault it is or isn't and concentrate on getting out of this mess?'

After a moments shocked silence Reg spoke up. 'I saw a film once where a plane crashed in the desert. The plane was wrecked but the survivors managed to build another plane out of the wreckage.'

'Yer, I saw that *Flight of the Phoenix*,' responded Norris. 'The original was way better.'

'Do you think? The effects were obviously better in the remake but I thought the acting was better too.'

'But the original definitely had more tension.'

'I hate to break up *Film Critic Weekly* but I presume there's a point to this?' Death hadn't seen the film and was worried that they would spoil the end.

'Well,' continued Reg. 'In the film they rebuild the plane into a smaller working plane. Maybe we could build a smaller car out of this one.'

'Right,' said Death dourly. 'And that's the best that you two can come up with? Build a smaller car, one that works presumably?'

Norris subtly pointed to Reg across his chest.

'It was his idea.'

'Well it was just a suggestion. Well not a suggestion as such, more of a moral booster. Just trying to highlight that a lot can be achieved if we work together. You know comrades together.'

'Maybe we should try cleaning the car?' Jenny offered.

'I don't really think giving Norris' car a quick wax is going to improve our situation,' snorted Death. 'But don't be disheartened, that's the best suggestion so far.'

'Don't be silly. I meant clean away all the sand. It's bound to have clogged up all the things in the engine... erm... like the carburettor?'

'Now that's what I'm talking about. Straight forward logical thought to get us out of this situation.' Death turned to Norris and Reg. 'See!'

Death popped open the bonnet up and they all crowded around the front of the car. He turned to

Jenny expectantly.

'So which bit is the carburettor?'

'Er I don't know. I thought you would.'

'Okay does anyone know which bit is the carburettor? Norris it's your car.'

'It's new. I haven't had a chance to familiarise myself with all the parts yet.'

'We could start with the plugs and points. It's those things there.' Reg pointed them out.

'We all know where the plugs are.' Norris felt slightly dejected by his lack of car knowledge, particularly in front of Jenny.

'It is rather sandy.' Jenny brushed the engine with her finger. 'Maybe we should just clean the whole thing, brush all the sand off. We're bound to get to the carburettor eventually.'

'Okay. Good. Let's get to work. You start brushing off the excess sand. Norris see if you can rustle up some old rags in the boot or something. Otherwise you guys will have to use your clothes. We need this engine clean. I'm going to look for some firmer sand where I might be able to get enough speed up to make a jump.'

'Er just one thing,' Norris didn't like interrupting people when they were being all efficient and official, (particularly when that person was generally referred to as the Grim Reaper) but he felt this was important. 'According to the S.A.S survival handbook, shelter and a source of water are the most important things in a desert survival situation. It increases your overall survival chances by eighty percent if you concentrate on these aspects first and foremost.'

'Wow really? Were you in the SAS?' Reg was impressed.

In fact they were all impressed. This lasted for about three seconds.

'Well no, but I saw a programme on it. Colonel Wayne *Mad Dog* McTavish's World of Extreme

Survival.'

Death looked at Norris, he would have given an apathetic sigh but he couldn't be bothered.

'Okay, what does Colonel Wayne *Mad Dog* McTavish suggest we do?'

'Well. Firstly, we need to obtain a source of water. Since there's no cactus plants to utilise, we can use an old sheet of polythene and a small hole dug in the sand.'

'How does that work?' Jenny had never seen World of Extreme Survival.

'Well any moisture in the ground condenses on the plastic and drips down into the cup below. Oh yeah, I'll need a cup or something too. And some rocks to secure the polythene. Oh and something to dig the hole with.'

'Shall I pop to the local shops to get these things? Gee, I hope they take cards, I haven't got any change on me.' Death patted his pockets to emphasise the point.

'Okay.' Norris muttered discontentedly. 'It was just a thought.'

'Shall I get some palm leaves and create some twine out of bamboo as well, so we can fashion a rudimentary ocean going vessel?'

'Actually, the interior of the car door will probably have polythene in it,' suggested Reg interrupting Death's tirade. 'Most cars have it, it stops water getting on the mechanism and rusting it.'

'And we can use the car ashtray to collect the water,' Jenny added excitedly. She liked the sound of the programme World of Extreme Survival and made a mental note to get someone to record it for her.

Norris was pleased that his idea was coming to fruition, but wasn't so happy about having the ashtray ripped out of his car and the doors pulled apart. His car was already looking worse for wear.

But as Colonel Wayne *Mad Dog* McTavish would often say; survival is sacrifice. Anyway, if they dismantled it carefully it should be easy to replace. The loud *crack* of snapping plastic broke his optimistic thoughts, as Death and Reg *carefully* tore the passenger door in half.

Less than twenty minutes later, Norris took a step back from his completed water producing device. He had to admit, although quietly and to himself, that he could have been in the special forces. Reg viewing the same contraption had to admit that Norris was going to die if they didn't get out of this. He hadn't just been standing round watching Norris work, that would have certainly been against his working class ethics. He had instead spent the time productively compiling an analysis of the region as a possible Hell. It had scored quite well; desolate, extremely hot and generally inhospitable. However, Reg predicted that transport issues may pose a significant hindrance to a smooth operational Hell. He therefore gave a preliminary eight and a half out of ten, providing that the transport network be improved. Jenny, who didn't have Reg's working class ethics, had in the same amount of time managed to clean a considerable amount of sand from the engine.

Death had managed to find a suitably flat and quite solid stretch of sand on which to make the jump. Granted it barely achieved the status of dirt track and certainly not road, but it would suit their purposes. Logistically however, it would be very difficult to get the Volvo there, as it required navigating an extremely large dune. He secretly wondered if it might be easier to wait for Norris to die and hitch a lift with the next Death that turned up.

By the time Death returned the sun had reached its apex and his companions were starting to look bedraggled. The extreme heat was starting to take its toll. Norris looked dejectedly at his water device. Despite the fact that his clothes were drenched through with perspiration, the ashtray had collected less liquid than a small fly could muster to spit contemptuously at his neighbour's choice of protein rich foods over sugar based products. Jenny had almost finished her work but still hadn't found the carburettor. Reg wandered over to Norris.

'Death's on his way back. How's it going?'

'I'm going to die out here.' Norris looked directly at Reg. 'I never really said it before. I'm really sorry I killed you. I, I never meant...'

'It's okay. I know you never meant to. And I'm sorry I dragged you into this mess. You know everyone thinks I brought you into this to get my revenge. I even convinced myself. But the truth is... I didn't have anyone else. I've got plenty of comrades, but no real friends, just people I know. So I picked you, so no-one would know. Pretty daft for a dead guy huh?'

There was an awkward moment's silence that Norris finally interrupted.

'What's it like being dead? I mean. I'm probably going to die and well, what's it like?'

'You're not Catholic are you?'

'No.'

'You'll probably like it then. I haven't been to Heaven yet but from all accounts it's a good place to be.'

'But what if Jesus doesn't want me for a sunbeam? I mean what about Hell?'

'It's awful.' Reg shuddered. 'And I was only a guest. You're not going to Hell though, you seem to be a stand up sort of guy.'

'I don't know, how strict are they?'

'Well it seems to be based on what you believe to be right and wrong in the most part. Obviously certain sins are punished no matter what. Like killing someone.'

'But I killed you. I'm going to Hell.'

'Yeah but that was an accident. And you apologised, so that won't count. Have you done anything else?'

'I did join the queue for ten items or less at the local supermarket when I clearly had twelve. I justified it by counting four tins of beans as one item in a multi-buy offer. Oh, how that is coming back to haunt me now.'

'They won't send you to Hell for that. I once took four items into the changing room at Fashion Man instead of three, and at the busiest time, they never mentioned that. Didn't buy from them either, capitalist scum were charging twenty pounds for a shirt, sixty percent polyester at that!'

Death had approached them silently and was listening in.

'Oh, Norris was just asking me all about death and the afterlife,' said Reg, finally noticing Death standing next to them.

'Oh, that's right,' said Death in a disgruntled voice. 'Go ask the guy with less than a week's experience. I've been dealing with death and the afterlife for nearly a millennium but what would I know about it.'

Death stormed off.

'What's up with him?' asked Norris. 'Bit touchy wasn't he?'

'He's under a lot of pressure at work. From what I can gather, his career hasn't been going that well. And now with all this.' Reg waved his hand around. 'I'll go and check he's alright.'

Norris watched Reg chase after Death. The small man's legs were struggling to keep up with the long strides of Death and every now and then he stopped to empty sand out of the turn-ups in his trousers. Under other circumstances he would have found the scene quite funny, but imminent death sort of affects an individual's sense of humour. Norris closed his eyes and listened to the sounds of the desert. Surprisingly, it wasn't as quiet as one might imagine. The sound of the wind blowing, the rustle of the shifting sands, and the deep throaty growl of a car's engine in the distance. Yep, Norris thought, you don't associate the sounds of the desert with a car engine. Ignoring his probable impending death he chuckled to himself, you certainly wouldn't expect that. Two seconds later Norris was running towards the others waving his hands in the air.

'Car! Car!'

'The desert madness has taken hold,' said Death wisely.

Norris stopped in front of them gasping for air. 'Car.'

'Yes,' said Reg tapping him sympathetically on the shoulder.

'No listen. I can hear a car.'

'It's probably a mirage.'

'I can hear it, not see it!'

'Well it's probably a mirage that you can hear rather than see. A hearing mirage.' Reg turned to Death 'You've probably heard of something like that before haven't you?'

'Wait, shh,' interrupted Jenny. 'I think he's right, listen!'

All four stood quietly. Sure enough the low rumble of a vehicle could distinctly be heard over the absence of any other really loud noise. As one, the four companions ran up a small dune towards the sound.

'There!' Jenny was the first to see the trailing sand cloud that indicated the vehicle's passage. 'Over here!' she shouted waving her arms.

'He'll never see us,' said Norris desperately.

'We need something to signal them with,' agreed

Reg.

'My mirror. We can use it to reflect the sun,' said Jenny, quickly emptying her handbag. 'Hold this.' She shoved a large leather, brass bound Bible towards Norris. The solid brass clasp dug into his chest.

'Ow. What do you have a Bible in your bag for?'

'I'm an Angel!' Jenny produced a tiny compact mirror.

'Is that it? We need something bigger.' Norris looked dolefully at the size of the mirror. 'That's miniscule.'

'I'm an Angel. A large mirror is a sign of vanity,' said Jenny, taking back her heavy brass bound Bible.

'The car!' Reg and Death yelled in unison, both running back to Norris' Volvo.

Jenny shoved the Bible back into her bag and attempted to signal the distant vehicle. She had to admit a larger mirror would be better, nevertheless it produced a sharp bright, blinking beam from its reflection of the sun. Norris turned to tell the others.

'Guys I think it'll be okay, this mirror is working fi...'

His sentence was cut off by the sight of Death and Reg on either side of his car kicking off the wing mirrors. Oh well, survival means sacrifice. They returned triumphantly with a wing mirror each. Reg passed Norris the rear view mirror.

'I brought you this.'

'They've seen us!' yelled Jenny with a little jump as the vehicle turned in their direction.

Their cheers and whoops lasted until the car, now recognisable as a Landrover, reached them in a cloud of dust and sand. All four ran to meet their would-be saviours. The driver jumped out with a hop, his loose, shoulder length blond hair taking a moment to catch up. The driver's rugged, sand-stained face broke into a smile.

'What's the bother?' he asked with a slight Australian accent. 'You on the rally or you just seriously lost?'

'We're lost,' replied Jenny. 'And the car is broken and we don't know how to fix it.'

The boys looked a bit dismayed by Jenny's straightforward approach to their predicament. A certain amount of masculine pride was required, no matter how dire the situation, if it had been any less so, they probably would have waved their rescuer on, claiming to have the situation under control. This however, was not really the same as being lost with a flat tyre on a camping trip in the lake district.

Norris quickly interjected. 'Yes, we seem to be having a spot of engine trouble. I think it's the carburettor.'

'No bother. My co here is an excellent mechanic.' The driver whistled. 'Jean-Claude see if you can fix up their car.'

Jean-Claude, the tall, skinny, and somehow obviously French co-driver quickly grabbed a tool box from the boot and followed Jenny to the car. The boys wandered slowly behind.

'Don't worry fellas if it's bust Jean-Claude can fix it, he's an excellent mechanic. Pity he's French. You have no idea how bloody irritating it is. He can't even say it, it's always *eet* with him. Four hundred miles of desert with everything being *eet* this *eet* that.'

As they got over the small dune Jean-Claude already had the bonnet up. Jenny stood next to him fascinated, as he tampered with the various components.

'Ah ha, eet is the carburettor, eet is kaput,' he shouted to them. 'Jean-Claude he will fix eet for you. Not a problem my friends.'

'See what I mean, bloody irritating. Worse thing

is I got to choose my co-driver. When I seen the name Jean on the list I thought that'll do for me. Well it's a woman's name ain't it, nice bit of skirt for those lonely desert nights. But oh no. Apparently it means John, what sorta country gives men bloody girl's names? The French that's who. Bloody pate eating drongos. Best co-driver I've had though hey. So you fellas are lost then?'

'Well we do seem to have got a bit disorientated,' whispered Death, pulling the driver out of the ear shot of Norris and Reg.

'Well it's quite simple hey, Paris is that way.' The Aussie pointed to his left. 'And Dakar is that way.'

'So you're on the Paris Dakar Rally.'

'No mate that rally got cancelled. We're doing the Paris Gnit Rally. Bit lesser known granted. Started in the eighties when Roy *Scotty* Campbell broke down just outside Dakar. He was in the lead by miles, so he claimed he won the Paris Gnit Rally rather than say he'd lost the Paris Dakar. Smart bloke if you ask me.'

'Ah ha. So we're in Africa then.'

The bewildered look Death received from the driver immediately informed him that he had accidentally spoken out loud.

'Cripes, you really are lost mate. Heard of a fella once got so lost he didn't know what country he was in. But never heard of anyone not knowing what continent they're in.'

Confusion over which country you are in, is in fact quite common. However, this is rarely attributed to being lost. It is more often a symptom of border disputes between two countries over who owns a certain tract of land; commonly referred to as war. This is not to be confused with land ownership. For example, when Britain amassed its gigantic empire it never once said that Britain as a country was spread half way across the world. It merely turned up and informed any local natives hanging around that their country now belonged to the British Empire. Most of the time the natives went along with this. Although the fact that the British generally brought lots of guns with them and most of the natives only had sharp sticks, may have had something to do with it. Perhaps the most famous example of not knowing which country you're in occurred in 1867 when the United States of America purchased Alaska from Russia for $7.2 million. Overnight the people of Alaska went from being Russian subjects to American. Imagine the Alaskans' confusion; they wouldn't have known what currency to use, what language to speak, or even what ice hockey team to support. Luckily, the United States didn't realise they were American until 1959, so they had plenty of time to adjust.

Death didn't have any such reason for not knowing what country he was in, so he relied on a lame excuse.

'It's your accent. I wasn't sure if we were still in Australia.'

The sound of an engine starting interrupted their conversation.

'Voila, eet is fixed,' shouted Jean-Claude.

Jenny gave him a kiss on the cheek, which Norris didn't take to well.

'Right let's tow you fellas onto the road. You should be good then hey.'

It took the remainder of the day to get the battered estate car onto solid ground. The stars were starting to break through the darkening purple sky as they said their goodbyes. Which, to Norris' further annoyance, involved Jean-Claude stealing another kiss from Jenny.

'Maybe we should find a hotel or something,' suggested Norris. 'I mean we're unlikely to get much of an idea about a place when it's dark like this.'

It had been a long day for Norris. He had started the day with an extremely beautiful girlfriend and a new career as a treasure hunter, but that had all changed, his whole world had crashed down before him. Of course, the crash had occurred long before he knew about it, but as far as he was concerned it had happened much later; when Reg and Death turned up at his doorstep. He was now faced with the fact, (and it was a fact, as much as he didn't want it to be) that he was travelling the world with Death and the ghost of the guy he'd killed, looking for a place to build a new Hell; added to which his girlfriend was an Angel, and he wasn't actually sure she was still his girlfriend. He had to admit he had acted quite badly when he'd found out. He'd make it up to her though. Maybe he'd take her bowling again, she seemed to like it. But right now all he wanted to do was lie on a comfortable bed and get his thoughts together.

'The day is not over yet I'm afraid,' replied Death.

'But it's dark.'

'It's not dark where we're going next.'

'Where's that?' asked Jenny

'The United States of America,' said Death dramatically waving his arms in the air as if the words were written above his head in neon lighting.

The other three didn't look so excited.

'America!' Death tried again this time raising his eyebrows as well. 'Huh, America. Come on it'll be fun. Maybe we can make a few side trips, see the sights.'

'Can we go tomorrow?' asked Norris. 'I'm a bit tired.'

Jenny and Reg nodded their agreement.

'Okay, to be honest with you, we're on a bit of a time scale here,' explained Death. 'I would imagine the amount of sinners is already stacking up and my job is kind of on the line. I'd like nothing more than to sit back with a couple of beers and chill, but well, I like my job. You get to meet all kinds of interesting people.'

'Okay. America it is.' Jenny's naturally kind nature meant she couldn't refuse someone who needed help.

'Yer,' said Norris, who didn't want to look like a lazy wimp in front of Jenny.

Realising that he was outvoted anyway Reg conceded in his own special way. 'Well I hope they pay overtime.'

'America,' repeated Death.

This time the others couldn't help giving a smile.

'So do you have to go to America much?' Reg questioned Death. He secretly hoped that a country so full of capitalists would be full of sinners.

'Well people die there just like other countries.'

Reg forgot that Death dealt with both sides in the eternal conflict.

'I mean do many Americans go to Hell?'

'No more than other places.' Death saw Reg's disappointment. 'But Hollywood, now that's a different matter.'

Reg brightened up.

'In fact,' continued Death. 'There's a whole department there just to deal with the *soul sellers*.'

'It's such a shame,' added Jenny. 'So many otherwise decent people signing on the dotted line for a bit of fame. There was a time when flashing your boobs was enough, but now they want so much more.'

The others looked shocked at Jenny's statement.

'What? I'm not that innocent,' declared Jenny defiantly. 'I've seen the world.'

'Okay then,' responded Death, with a slightly sarcastic tone. 'Let me just get my bearings with the stars, then it's America.'

Death stared up at the night sky pretending to take reference from various constellations, just like he imagined the ancient mariners would have done. Above him the stars shone brightly, like tiny moth bitten holes in the curtain of night.

'Well there's Mortis Minor and Andromedus is beyond the Northern Callipers. So Paris is that way.' Death pointed in the direction that he'd been told earlier.

Death was pleased with the suitably impressed expressions his subterfuge received.

'So which way is America?' asked Jenny.

Bugger. Death realised the slight flaw in his subterfuge.

'Well, er. Geographically speaking it should be that way.' Death pointed.

He did know the rough direction of America and figured it was pretty big and shouldn't be that hard to miss. His attitude mirrored that of Christopher Columbus who figured much the same. Pick a direction keep going and you're bound to end up reaching land eventually, and if anyone asks, just tell them you're following the stars.

'Okay here we go,' Death remarked positively.

With a slight rev of the engine Death spun the car in the direction of America and slammed on the brakes. The car skidded to a halt sending a spray of sand from the wheels.

'Er, is America supposed to look like this?' enquired Reg. 'I mean is it supposed to look so sandy and Sahara Desert like.'

'And dark, it's daytime in the USA, isn't it?' added Norris.

'Okay slight hitch. No problem.'

Death tried again. He hit the brakes so hard this time that the car spun one hundred and eighty degrees before jerking to a stop. Before anyone had the chance to comment Death quickly tried again, with much the same result.

'Okay problem. I can't stop quick enough. The sand is giving way under the wheels.'

'You mean we're stuck here.' Norris feared he may yet die in this bleak wilderness.

'No. It's fine, I've just got to re-evaluate our stopping process.'

'How are we going to do that? What do you suggest?' Fear now gripped Norris.

Death pointed to a slight mound of rock protruding from the sand.

'I suggest that rocky outcrop over there. Seat belts on!'

'What do you mean?' asked Norris as Death sped towards the outcrop. 'Oh. No, wait a sec. Surely we can...'

The car stopped before Norris could finish his sentence.

Chapter 14

Elle Bradley sat in the boardroom of the Houston office. In front of her, spread out across the long polished table lay the blueprints for the all new Hell. The design had been commissioned a few months previously, how he'd known it would be needed she didn't know, and wasn't stupid enough to ask. She'd already checked over them several times, but this was an important meeting and Elle liked to be prepared. She had to admit, the plans were impressive, designed by the ground breaking Scandinavian architect and interior designer, Jurgen Jungstrom.

Jungstrom had been a prominent advocator of the ergonomic school of design. In fact he'd been the pre-eminent designer for the movement, culminating in his *comfortable living project*. The homes he created were at the apex of ergonomics. Jurgen designed every aspect of the new houses; from their interior designs, to their locations. The houses were so perfect that workmen were often led away weeping from the completed buildings they could never afford to live in. Later, many of them had had to receive counselling for post building stress disorder.

However, not long after the housing went on the market a few shortcomings were discovered. The problem was that the houses were ergonomically perfect; too ergonomically perfect. The home-owners' found them so comfortable that they lost all desire to actually leave them. They soon found themselves slowly becoming socially inept, as they distanced themselves from the outside world. Worse still, many hosted house warming parties and found it next to impossible to get the guests to depart, eventually having to turn to costly court cases and eviction orders. The main problem however, came months later. The houses were expensive and the buyers relied on well paid jobs to afford them. Well paid jobs that they lost for not turning up to work, because the houses were too comfortable to leave. The whole thing became a disaster for Jungstrom; nobody wanted his houses anymore. They were just too nice.

At this point many a man would have given it all up, but not Jurgen Jungstrom. He learnt from his mistakes, and so he founded the anti-ergonomic movement. Jungstrom became a multi-millionaire almost overnight with his new uncomfortable and awkward to live in houses and apartments.

Businessmen soon spotted the advantage of not actually wanting to go home, and therefore being able to put in those extra hours in work. Prices for his ergonomically deficient houses sky rocketed, many seeing the advantage of owning one as a second, or holiday, home. After all, who would want to take a time off work and pay out money to go on a holiday in a house like that. Eventually his anti-ergonomic designs became so perfect that the housing had to be sold at a minimum distance of five hundred yards to avoid sickness.

As Elle looked at the blueprints she had to admit Jungstrom had designed a Hell that not even the hardiest sinner would want to live in. With a quick glance at her diamond studded watch, she folded up the blueprints and pressed the intercom button.

'You can send them in now.'

In the adjoining waiting room the mechanical echoing of Elle's voice reached past the dutiful secretary to the ears of those waiting. Two rows of seats stretched along the opposite walls parallel to the secretary's desk, giving an almost bench like appearance to the seating arrangements. The secretary looked up through her obligatory glasses at the scene. It reminded her of a group of naughty school children waiting to be summoned to the headmistress' office. Only the assembled twelve men and one woman were not naughty school children. They were amongst the most powerful men (and woman) in the world. Not powerful in the sense that they could walk alone, down a poorly lit inner city street, without fear of having their mobile phones taken from them by two hooded youths using poor grammar in their request. They were powerful in the business sense of the word.

They walked in a disgruntled manner into the boardroom; they were not used to being treated like this. For them, business meetings usually involved a free lunch. In fact, they were so used to this etiquette that the majority of them had long forgotten how to feed themselves. Following a general consensus however, none of them spoke out in complaint. They just filed in like they *were* naughty school children, under the gaze of Headmistress Bradley. Granted, they were all powerful in the business world, but in that world Elle Bradley also had a reputation and nobody messed with her. It was also rumoured that she had a reputation in the inner city world too, and that hooded youths often went home to mummy, crying that their trainers had been taken.

'Please take a seat.' Elle opened her arms as an invitation to the seats running down the long table. 'In front of you is a business proposal, I will give you a moment to browse through it.'

In front of each of them lay a neatly presented folder which they began to flick through. Elle didn't feel the need to give a presentation. Everything that they needed to know was written within the folders, and these people had been given the privilege of an education in some of the top schools and universities, it therefore followed, that they should be able to read. As they read, she watched them slowly and furtively look around to see each other's responses. She had expected this. She knew what they'd think. They were probably right now wondering where the hidden cameras were. Any second now some television presenter is going to jump out and say some zany catch phrase like *you've been cajoled*. And they'll laugh along not caring that they've been made to look complete idiots in front of millions of viewers. Eventually, one of them gave an attention seeking cough.

'Mr Johnston?'

Mr Johnston described himself as a venture capitalist, the law courts described him as a tax evader twice acquitted. He rose slightly from his seat, revealing his well proportioned body; well proportioned in the sense that it was proportioned slightly too large to be aesthetically pleasing.

'This is some kind of joke right?'

'Oh no. I assure you this is no joke. I never joke about money.'

'Hell? I mean Hell, as in the Bible. Here on Earth?'

'Oh yes. If you'd care to look at the contracts, my company has written an insurance pay-out if any of this is false.'

The others looked at the extremely generous pay out offer with gleaming eyes, but Mr Johnston was not to be swayed.

'No disrespect, but I think you're crazy. There ain't no Heaven and there certainly ain't no Hell.' He took his belief in atheism religiously. 'Now if you don't mind I think it's time for me to leave.'

Elle wasn't a fool. She knew this was almost impossible to believe. It was for this reason she'd arranged to provide a little convincer, but Johnston had annoyed her. She didn't need him and that was a very dangerous place to be, it made him disposable.

'Iscyrus, would you be so kind as to see Mr Johnston out.'

Everyone flinched as Iscyrus suddenly appeared from the shadows in the far corner of the room. No-one had noticed him before. With a silent sweeping movement he moved to the door, and opened it. Johnston gave an involuntary nervous gulp and left with Iscyrus close behind. The door closed with a finality. Elle made a mental note to send flowers of condolence to the Johnston family in the morning.

'Now of course I realise many of you will be feeling the same as Mr Johnston, but before you make a decision, allow me to introduce my partner in this venture. I'm sure he'll be able to convince you that this is a genuine proposal.'

The room was suddenly filled with a loud cracking sound, like the slapping of leather in a private room downstairs in a seedy Dutch brothel (one would imagine). Chairs toppled and bodies fell over each other as the potential investors clambered for the furthest wall away from the fearful sight of Bacchaus, who had appeared out of nothingness. Although appearing in Demon form did make him conspicuous, he had to admit he did like to make an entrance. He flexed and stretched his enormous leathery wings, cricked his neck to the right, and smiled as the smell of recently dispensed urine reached his nostrils. The money held little interest for him, these pitiful little souls merely aided his subterfuge, he could hide behind their greed. He spread out his wings and rose to his full height, nearly thirteen foot (he'd always been tall for his age).

'DO ANY OF YOU DOUBT ME?'

Then with another loud bang Bacchaus was gone. Although he wasn't the type to stay and chat, he had little choice in having to leave so quickly. Rules governed the amount of time he could spend on Earth, particularly in his true form; rules that not even he could break. The longer he spent on Earth the weaker his powers became. Even with such a short visit his full powers were restricted, and that made him vulnerable. He didn't like being vulnerable, it just wasn't fitting for a Demon of his standing.

It took Elle nearly an hour and a half raiding her drinks' cabinet to get everyone calmly sitting back at the table. Luckily, these were powerful men (and woman) in the business world and they'd got there through greed, and greed was on the menu.

It is written that it is easier for a camel to pass through the eye of a needle than for a rich man to enter Heaven. At face value it would therefore appear that the wealthy don't get to go to Heaven. However, a number of possible solutions have been presented. For example, some bright spark pointed out that the *eye of the needle* was the nickname for a secret entrance to Jerusalem used by traders. Other solutions have suggested that; you can't take riches with you so you are technically poor when you die, that the very rich could buy a huge needle or a very small camel, and all you need is a hacksaw and an industrial liquidiser. The latter, has been almost universally dismissed by theologians. Disregarding the evidence that appeared before them, few at the meeting considered the prospect of not getting into Heaven. Universally, they figured that a quick donation to some charity should absolve them of all sinful discretions, a solution widely approved of by wealthy theologians. As the prospect of the vast riches to be made took hold of her audience, Elle continued.

'As I'm sure you're beginning to realise, the potential of this venture is great. Some of you are here purely as investors, others of you will be interested in business franchises. Let me start by saying that we predict a considerable revenue from the tourist market. You will notice a Hell themed amusement park on the outskirts, this will be no mouse run organisation like others I can mention. (A few laughs broke out amongst the potential investors). We plan to run helicopter trips over Hell and naturally, guided tours, but that is just the start. Imagine the possibilities if you will, stag and hen weekends, visiting recently deceased relatives, and, my favourite, weddings. Imagine the fun of being able to say you were married in Hell; this marriage was made in Hell. I'm sure you'll realise the sort of people who this would be attractive to, look at the popularity of Elvis themed weddings in Vegas. Well this has even more potential. Of course, there's also the merchandise. Postcards from Hell - wish you were here, key rings and the usual tat. And obviously T-shirts; I love Hell, my parents went to Hell and all I got was this lousy T-shirt. We're presently in negotiations with a toy manufacturer to bring out a line of action figures, with all your favourite sinners and Demons, each with their own small imp carrying a large whip. There are also a number of vacant lots available for those of you interested in a franchise, with some prime sites availa....'

Elle's speech was interrupted by two portly gentlemen at the far end of the table. Their rivalry in the fast food market spilled into the meeting as their raised voices drew everyone's attention.

'Just because your company claims to have fire burnt burgers doesn't mean you should have exclusive rights to Hell,' said Mr Hobson, a slightly larger man in a black suit.

Mr Renwold's face reddened and blotched in irritation.

'I was just saying you're more suitable to the Heaven market, with your so called heavenly arches theme going on.'

'You just want a monopoly on Hell. But I do agree that your burgers are from Hell.'

At this point Mr Renwold launched himself at Mr Hobson, causing him to fall back from his seat. Hobson laying splayed on the floor, struck out with a series of kicks, preventing his rival from getting close enough to finish him off. Eventually, Renwold dived on the prone man, and the fight deteriorated into two fat men rolling on the floor trying to hit, butt, and bite each other in a vain attempt to cause as much damage as possible. Watching the scene Elle smiled. It didn't take a business genius to realise she wasn't going to have trouble getting investment in the project.

Chapter 15

The Volvo estate slid to a stop. It took a moments blinking for the car's occupants' eyes to adjust; they had travelled from night sky to daylight in, well the blink of an eye really.

'Phew. I thought you were going to drive into that boulder.' Norris was a touch disorientated but relieved.

'I did,' said Death.

The crumpled bonnet of the previously good value, second-hand buy Volvo confirmed this. Norris jumped out of the car and slid to the front to examine the damage. He turned to the others with tears in his eyes. It was hard to tell whether the tears were from anguish or from excessive blinking, but he did look upset.

'You've killed my car!'

'It's just a little bit of cosmetics,' said Death, slipping erratically as he joined Norris. 'Just need to pull the bumper up a bit.'

Death pulled at the front valance, trying to pull it back to where the car's manufacturer had originally intended it to be. With a supreme effort and a loud *snap* the last remaining bolt gave up its valiant struggle and the bumper came completely off. He casually handed it to Norris.

'You've got insurance right?'

'I haven't even finished paying the finance on it yet,' retorted Norris, looking at the bumper in his hand.

Reg came around to the front of the vehicle with the wobbling gait of someone struggling with unsure footing.

'Well I must commend you on your choice of automobile. Very good safety features, nobody was hurt. Most cars would have just crumpled with that sort of impact.'

Norris stood looking despondently at his car. His previously shiny pride and joy now looked like the loser in a stock car race. Jenny joined them with the grace of an ice skater.

'Hey come on, deep sea treasure hunters don't need Volvo estates.'

'I was going to part exchange it for a boat.'

Reg gave a little cough to gain their attention.

'Er, as much as I sympathise with your current plight comrade, I do believe we may have a slightly more er, pressing problem. Is anyone feeling cold?'

'Well now that you mention it. I'm freezing. What the...' Norris looked around for the first time.

The surrounding scenery could best be described as white. Although the reflected light gave a patchy presence of blue, and the odd spot of black was also scattered around randomly, it was white. The kind of intense white that is best achieved by a nuclear blast. The companions stood shivering in the midst of a vast icy tundra.

'I don't think this is America.' Reg turned stating the obvious into an art form.

'I think we must be at one of the Poles,' stated Death sagely.

'Oh great. You've wrecked my car and got us lost... Again,' complained Norris.

'We're not lost. I told you we're at one of the Poles.'

'But which one? They are pretty far apart you know. You might even say they're polar opposites.'

'I know how we can find that out,' said Reg triumphantly.

The others turned expectantly towards Reg.

'Well the North Pole has polar bears and the South Pole has penguins.'

Death gave a slight sigh.

'Do you see any polar bears?' he asked.

'No.'

'Do you see any penguins?'

'Er, no,' said Reg, realising the flaw in his logic.

'How about Father Christmas? I hear he hangs out at the North Pole.'

'Okay point taken. So how are we going to get out of this one?'

'It's not a problem. It happens all the time.'

'Wwwhat happens all the tttime? Ending up at one of the poles on your way to America.' Norris highlighted the word America imitating Death's earlier arm waving gesture. The cold always made him grumpy. 'Wwwhat happened this tttime? Has one of those guiding ssstars moved?'

'Look it's simple. I just miscalculated slightly. I'm pretty sure I know where I went wrong. We've just got to go back the way we came. We'll just put the car in reverse and I'll re-alter our direction.'

'Bbbut how are we going to move? The car wwwill never get a ggrip on thisss ice.'

Death scanned the region.

'Simple. We'll push the car over to that slight decline, over there. Then we can stop using that ice mound at the bottom.'

Reg took out his notebook.

'Just one thing, before we leave maybe we should consider this place as a suitable Hell. I mean the cold can be as bad as extreme heat.'

'I hhhave tto agggree,' said Norris, his words stumbling out of his now distinctly blue lips.

Death considered Reg's suggestion for a brief moment, not out of any real deliberation, but more because he found Norris' blue lips amusing.

'Won't work,' he said finally.

'Why not?'

'Well it would mean that Hell was in fact frozen over. Can you imagine the pandemonium that would cause? Anyone who has ever said I'll do it when Hell freezes over, would actually have to do it. Because in essence Hell would be frozen over and that's the rules. For one, Francesca Newbody would have to sleep with me. Can you imagine that?'

'Oh.' Reg slotted his book back in his pocket, and tried his best not to imagine that.

'Actually, come to think of it that might not be such a bad idea,' mused Death smiling to himself.

'Can wwe gggo nnow?'

'I just want to check...' began Death, but a glare from Jenny interrupted him. 'Yer sure better had.'

Death climbed into the driver's seat as the others positioned themselves around the bonnet to push the car backwards. With much slipping and sliding the car began to move slowly towards the ice mound.

'Okay we're moving now, everyone get in before the momentum picks up. Once we're going I won't be able to stop.'

They didn't need a second invitation to get inside. Reg and Norris even conceded to let Jenny have the front seat. Not through any gallant gesture, but through the fear that a squabble could ultimately leave them both stranded behind. The car rapidly descended towards the ridge.

'Hold on everybody!' warned Death.

The car stopped with a sudden explosion of ice and snow.

The Volvo estate appeared in front of a large rusty looking boulder. The boulder's chosen residence was one of a sparse arid landscape, although other boulders shared the vicinity, they were few and far between. The majority of the occupied space was filled with dirt and small scrub bushes.

Death gave his customary wide grinned smile to his companions. 'Told you it wasn't a problem. We're back in the civilised world.'

'Doesn't look like there's much in the way of

civilisation to me,' said Reg, looking out at barren landscape surrounding them.

'That's civilisation for you. Just pops up when you least expect it.'

'So this is America?' asked Norris.

'Yes it is,' confirmed Death. 'Not sure where in America though.'

Norris gave a slight chuckle as a smile broke across his face.

'You know what, who cares where in America we are. I'm actually having the time of my life. This is a real adventure. About the biggest risk I'd taken before all this was crossing the road before the green man said I could. And now, I've been fighting for survival stranded in a desert, involved in a bar room brawl, stuck in a frozen wasteland on one of the poles, still don't know which one, and to top it all, shot at. This is amazing. And guess what? I'm still alive!'

'Oooh, I'm still alive. Lucky you!' said Reg in good humoured banter, waving his arms around in mock celebration.

The four occupants of the car erupted into laughter, as the stress of the day's events lifted. They had faced adversity together and that had bonded them in a friendship that few would ever understand. As Reg would say, they were comrades. Or as Death would say, they were people that I hung out with once.

'Now this is what I'm talking about,' said Death, driving the car on to what appeared to be a track weaving between the boulders and shrubs. 'Let's go find Hell.'

Despite the upbeat mood of its occupants, the car refused to join in. It chugged along the nearby dirt track that Death had spotted, giving an occasional splutter and jerk in complaint. Try as it might, the car had little effect on the atmosphere within and it wasn't long before a sing song started, with most of the words remembered and in the correct order.

People often comment that somebody or other has the voice of an Angel. It is however, most probable, that they do not have Jenny in mind when they utter this phrase. If they do have Angel Jenny in mind they are in fact saying; her voice is adequate but despite the formal choral training that most Angels undergo, she is still missing many of the crucial notes. If they are however, referring to the soloist from a local school nativity play, they probably have got Jenny in mind.

Luckily, this made little difference to the overall performance bellowing out from the car. Her voice harmonised perfectly with the boys' equally inadequate renditions. They had barely enough time to create a compilation CD of classic sing along car tunes before Reg broke away from the cacophony.

'Shh. Over there! Is that a road?'

Since early Roman times roads have been easily identifiable, mostly due to their relatively flat, straight, and long qualities, and their ability to make land travel easier. The vast majority of people soon learnt what a road was, and how to recognise one. (Thereby providing yet another example of the human's superiority over the hedgehog). In line with mankind's inability to keep life simple, it was deemed that roads were far too easy to recognise. An effective solution was presented; the naming of individual roads. Man was now free to get confused and ask random strangers questions about the road. Such as, 'is this the A432 towards Chipping Sodbury?' Whereas, previously, it would have been unthinkable to ask a stranger 'is this a road?' As quite obviously, both participants in the conversation would have known the answer.

In his defence, Reg's question had little to do

with an inability to recognise a road. He'd been able to recognise roads from an early age, even before his mother had told him to go and play on them. His question was more to do with the distance and obscured nature of the road.

'I think you're right,' replied Death, who was also quite adept at recognising roads, particularly the long, straight ones.

The dirt track they were travelling on appeared to be running parallel to the road. Death made a hard turn. The dust cloud that the car created increased ten fold as they left the track. It billowed out from all sides of the Volvo, surrounding it in a gritty yellow mist. The missing windows allowed the sandy dirt to fill the car; putting an end to the passengers' singing and causing them to choke and splutter, mirroring the noise of the struggling car's engine. As they reached the road Death pulled over to allow them all to brush the dirt off themselves.

'Genuine Armani, why do I bother?' he muttered under his breath, as he tried to rid his suit of the sticking dust. 'Okay, left or right?'

The road stretched out long and straight in both directions with no recognisable landmarks or signs. They clambered back in the car, no-one committing to a decision.

Death turned to Norris with one last brush of his shoulder. 'Which way? Pick one.'

'Well left I guess.'

Death turned right.

'Er, I said left. We're going right.'

'Yep. I figured last time you made a decision on which way to go you killed someone.'

There was a moment's silence to Death's remark before Reg spoke up.

'Well you really can't deny that one,' he said chuckling.

'Okay. Okay,' said Norris, taking the good humoured laughter aimed at his expense.

As the journey continued on the seemingly endless road, the conversation in the car slowly dropped off, leaving the passengers to fidget and shift restlessly in their seats, looking out at the monotonous dry landscape. It wasn't exactly an uncomfortable silence, more a boring one, where you've run out of interesting things to say; the sort of silence you rarely get when you're alone. After about an hour Jenny finally spoke.

'How about a game of *I spy*?'

'Road, sky, desert, sand.' Death didn't want to play.

'Actually I was going to say *m*, for those mountains we're heading towards.'

It was a lie, she was going to say *r* for road. She justified her lie by the fact that she would have eventually said *m* for mountains, so technically it wasn't a lie, albeit, after she'd done sky, desert, and sand as well.

'What about *s* for that signpost up ahead?' said Norris excitedly.

'You're supposed to wait until we guess, silly. Doesn't anyone know how to play?' Jenny was a bit upset, she loved *I spy*.

'No, signpost, as in we can find out where we are and where we're heading. Maybe there's a town.'

Death slowed down as they approached the signpost, giving them ample opportunity to read the weather beaten words.

Come see the World's Biggest Ball of String.

Incorporated with the String Museum and seasonal tour.

Also this is your last chance to get fuel for miles, so you're going to have to stop at:-

Al's Petroleum Emporium. Take the first left.

Jenny bobbed up and down in her seat with enthusiasm.

'Can we go? I reckon it'll be fun. The World's

biggest ball of string imagine that.'

All three passengers looked at Death with bated breath. He looked at the petrol gauge; they did need fuel.

'Yer, why not. I did promise we could see the sites. And I guess we can spare the time.'

Secretly, Death had already decided that Australia would do as Hell. He was already getting tired of the travelling around. Besides he liked the poetic element of using Australia mainly because of Barcroft Boake's *Where Dead Men Lie*. Although not really the type to attend poetry recitals, Death did have a distinctive taste when it came to poetry. He enjoyed verse that had a morose and dark quality. He also quite liked *The Owl and the Pussy Cat*.

Whether it was the excitement of visiting the String Museum or the misconception of the distance involved, it didn't seem long before they arrived at the left turn. A short way along stood a ramshackle group of buildings which with some pomposity proclaimed itself a town. The town of Little Merit, as the sign informed them, stood at an elevation of 4215 ft and had a population of 59. A population that would be safe from any flood below 4200 ft, as the sign further informed any visitors; most likely in an attempt to encourage more settlers or businesses. Attached to the bottom of the sign by two short chains hung a wooden placard: Greater Merit only has an elevation of 4157 ft.

They pulled into the dusty gravel strewn car park designated for patrons of the String Museum only! The only other vehicle in the lot was a large, white motor home, slightly discoloured but in otherwise good condition. A large man whose size probably had more to do with his diet of fatty meat based cuisine than his claim of being big boned, hurried along his small in number but large in size family. The family consisted of the man, his wife and a beach ball they called son. The beach ball's attention was largely centred on greedily consuming an overly sized ice cream, which despite his efforts, was rapidly escaping his mouth and running down his thick fingered hand. The woman was attempting to join them by exiting the front seat as demurely as possible; which in her case involved hitching up her billowing flowery skirt, revealing rippling mounds of upper thigh. The motor home almost heaved a sigh of relief as she left and its suspension sprung up several inches.

The four left the Volvo and followed the oversized family through the entrance of the String Museum. At the counter stood a skinny man whose hair had long since given up its struggle to cover the top of his head. He had not however given up the effort and combed the last remaining strands sideways over the balding top. Reg self consciously touched the back of his head where he'd noticed his own balding patch. Maybe it was lucky he'd died when he had, he thought to himself. The skinny proprietor gave a weak smile, revealing an inadequate number of teeth.

'You're just in time for the next tour. Five dollars each.'

'Frank Jr's a half,' said the large man, putting his sweat soaked hands into his checked shorts for his wallet.

The proprietor raised an eyebrow quizzically. Frank Jr. raised his head up from the business of licking the remaining ice cream from the gaps in his fingers, and smiled.

'Thirteen dollars then.'

Death followed and paid the twenty dollars, insisting it was his treat, whilst pocketing the receipt for his expense form B6219.

The seven tourists entered the large, barn-like structure that housed the *World's Largest Ball of String*. Little in life can prepare you for the magnitude of a large ball of string. You can look at a regular ball of string and imagine it a lot bigger, or even imagine yourself a lot smaller and standing next to it, but nothing really prepares you for a genuinely large ball of string. They all nodded appreciatively as the tour guide entered from a side door; it certainly was a large ball of string. She was a pretty girl, with large brown eyes and dark brown hair tied back in an official businesslike manner. She smiled pleasantly at each of the patrons. A slight touch of pink in her cheeks was the only outward sign of her nervousness as she proceeded into her well rehearsed repertoire.

'The ancient philosopher Confucius once asked, how long is a piece of string? Well in this case I can tell you, it's 7,827,804 feet and 8 inches long. That's nearly 1,500 miles long. If we unwound it, it would stretch from here to Houston, Texas. That's long enough to wrap eight million average sized presents. The word string itself comes from the old English word streng, which in itself derives from the Germanic word strang; the word for strong. And string certainly is strong. Its strength comes from taking numerous strands and twisting them together. Incidentally, the word twine comes from the word for two. The aboriginal Butowana tribe believe that the world was created by the Great String Maker, who bound the masculine and feminine with a bit of string he found in the back of the drawer where he kept his tea towels. Whether, this is how life truly began, it's difficult to say, but we cannot deny that string has had an important role in shaping the world as we know it...'

The guide's speech continued well beyond her audience's attention span. The visitors began to wander around, looking at the various exhibits surrounding the colossal ball of string. Death, Norris and Reg all pretended to be particularly interested in a glass case containing a "genuine bit of string, owned by George Washington."

'Any questions?' asked the guide.

Jenny who had listened rapturously to the guide's talk, raised her hand.

'That is amazing, is that really the world's biggest ball of string?'

'Er... well... um.' Something was preventing the guide from lying. The pressure was building up inside her, the others had all turned their attention to her now. Cracks in the facade appeared, suddenly she burst out. 'I can't do this anymore! It's not true! The biggest ball of string is in Cawker City, Kansas. We're not even the second biggest.'

The guide burst into tears. Death watched as she ran out, then turned to face the flabbergasted Angel.

'Nice one Jenny, now I'll never find out what George Washington used his string for.'

'But... but. I only asked.'

The large man beckoned to his family.

'Come on. We're not staying here.'

He stormed out, his family close behind him.

Death smiling, clapped his hands together in a businesslike fashion.

'Well it's been fun, but I guess we'd better get back to work.'

On their way out they passed the large man, his face now purple and blotchy, as he confronted the proprietor.

'I demand my money back! I didn't pay to see any old big ball of string. I paid to see the largest!'

Death paused as they passed the complaining family.

'He's got a point, maybe I should....'

'Let's just go.' Jenny was looking decidedly sheepish. 'Poor girl, I hope she's okay.'

'Well you should have realised it's really hard to lie to an Angel.'

'I didn't know she was lying. It was an awfully large ball of string,' said Jenny as they climbed back into the car. 'It's a pity, I wanted to get something from the gift shop for my friend Lucy.'

They drove out of Little Merit along the road on which they had entered the ramshackle town. Little did they marvel at the wonder of the road that not only allowed you to enter but also to leave. The dual purpose of roads is often overlooked or just plain taken for granted. As the old adage says; all roads lead to Rome. It must therefore, be equally true that all roads lead from Rome, yet seemingly this doesn't even warrant a footnote. Not until you are faced with an unfamiliar inner city one way system does this beneficial phenomenon become truly appreciated. Yes Winchester City Borough, I'm talking about you!

A short distance away from the museum, Death pulled the car over to the side of the road.

'Bugger, I forgot to get petrol.' He gave a quick look over his shoulder before attempting a U-turn. 'Typical. No cars for miles, then when I need to make a turn.'

He drew their attention to two cars rapidly approaching them from the rear. The almost identical SUV's advanced with a certain degree of menace. The menace was largely achieved by their appearance. Both were black, with matching blacked out windows, the deep polish scarred with yellow desert dust along the lower sills. Had they been lilac they would have been considerably less menacing and more likely to be used to pick up the kids after school. They were the sort of vehicles you'd imagine Secret Service operatives using, if they didn't want to be secret and wanted people to think *Oh there goes the Secret Service*. In unison, the two SUV's skidded to a sideways halt either end of the Volvo effectively blocking it in.

'Could be trouble.' Death didn't think they were being used for the school run.

The front passenger door of the lead vehicle

opened, and out stepped a *strategically shaved gorilla* in a dark suit. His name was Hans Von Gruber, a man with short cropped blond hair, blue eyes and a chiselled physique. His huge physical presence had always dominated his intellect. Throughout his school years teachers had neglected him academically; he was built for sports after all, and that was where his talent should lie. Now if he'd been small, skinny and wearing glasses, well maybe there'd have been a chance for him.

Hans opened the rear passenger door. The man who stepped out was small, skinny and wore glasses. He'd received every academic privilege available. His name was Kurt Becker, but no-one in *The Organisation* called him Kurt, he was always Mr Becker. Yes, he definitely commanded respect within *The Organisation*. His physical appearance made it quite obvious that he wasn't the muscle and therefore must be the brains. Recently, Mr Becker had begun to worry about *The Organisation*. Quite frankly, he began to wonder if it was in fact, evil. Growing up as a child he'd never pictured himself as a baddie. But he'd seen enough films to know that everything pointed to his employers being well, the bad guys. They employed the muscle like Hans, they drove around in black SUV's, and referred to themselves as *The Organisation*.

'They're going to kill us, well again I mean,' said Reg.

'No, I don't think so,' said Norris with a sudden blast of female intuition. (Well it would be quite sexist to think that only women should have exclusive rights over the whole female intuition thing). 'I think they're here to offer us some sort of deal.'

Mr Becker walked briskly to the car.

'Gentlemen, and lady of course.' He gave a slight inclination of his head in a gesture of respect. 'My employer would like a word. If of course, it's not too much of an inconvenience?'

The looming presence of Hans behind him made it a surety that no request would be too much of an inconvenience. Mr Becker took their lack of response as a sign that they were willing to comply.

'Good. If you'd like to step out of the vehicle. Miss Bradley will be joining us shortly.'

'What does Miss Bradley want with us?' Jenny asked Becker, breaking the brief moment of feet shuffling silence, as they all stood beside the Volvo.

'I think it's better that I let her explain. Ah, here she is now.'

They looked both left and right down the long expanse of empty road. Becker gave a slight cough to draw their attention and pointed skyward. In the distance a small speck was expeditiously taking shape as it drew nearer. The dark outline of a helicopter was soon clearly distinguishable, and the rumbling vibration of its passage reached their ears. Typical capitalist ostentatiousness thought Reg as he voiced an opinion.

'Well your employer certainly travels in style.'

'Yes, it's the Westland Lynx. Finest small passenger helicopter in the world. At 262 km per hour it holds still the air speed record for any helicopter. Well at least until the new Skviorsky is fully tested and on the market.'

Reg wasn't really expecting a pseudo intellectual discussion about helicopters with Becker. He was more or less expecting a *yes she does* response, but he knew a few things about helicopters too. Well, one thing anyway.

'Leonardo Da Vinci invented the helicopter.'

Of course, this is really a matter of opinion. The same opinion would lead you to believe that Da Vinci also invented the submarine, parachute and probably the electric toaster as well. The basis for this is a series of sketches' showing such inventions and not actual working models. In which case I invented the first super-hyper space rocket ship aged nine, and my sketch was in colour too.

It was at this point that everyone decided it was probably best to go back to the feet shuffling silence and just wait for the Westland Lynx to arrive; which thankfully for them all was not too long a wait. A whirlwind of sand sprang up around the helicopter as it touched down, making everyone duck their heads and cover their faces with their hands. The side door of the jet black Lynx slid back and Becker led them forward. Once inside, the door was slammed shut and the helicopter sprang into the air, barely giving them time to fall back into their seats.

Regardless of his apparent in-depth knowledge of helicopters Reg had never actually flown in one. He quickly joined the others in fastening his seat belt, even though he was dead he still feared for his life. Flying had always made him nervous. On a package holiday to the Costa Del Sol, he'd insisted on having a seat in the rear of the aircraft. His logic for this was simple; he'd never heard of a plane reversing into a mountain. If planes were bad, helicopters were even worse, at least planes had wings. Things that fly have wings, things that don't, just fall. To him the helicopter was just falling differently to the other things without wings. Sooner or later though, it would inevitably end the same way as everything else without wings. It would hit the ground... hard. He figured the only reason they were staying in the air was because no-one had actually pointed out that the helicopter should have wings, so he kept his thoughts to himself, just in case.

The thoughts of the other companions were largely dominated by the mysterious Miss Bradley, whose presence was missing from the luxurious beige interior.

The difference between luxurious beige and

ordinary household beige is one of subtle shading. Only the most discerning of tastes could have picked the shade used in the helicopter interior, but the difference was recognisable by all who viewed it. It wept of taste and money (a combination so rarely mixed). This view was reinforced by the soft, cushioned, leather seats. The leather itself was provided by cattle kept away from wire fencing or anything else that could nick or mar their precious hides. Hides which were moisturised daily with cocoa butter creams. In essence, they were raised and pampered on a cattle health farm. The result delivered the sort of seats that make you realise what you've been missing in your own seating arrangements; the pure, unadulterated pleasure that sitting down can provide. No punch line, these were just damn good seats!

As the aircraft levelled, a host appeared from a small sectioned off compartment at the rear. He wore an immaculate navy blue suit and carried a silver tray with four full champagne glasses on it, which he handed to the guests. As Norris took his glass he figured his intuition had been right; nobody would go to this much trouble if they intended to cause them harm. Norris didn't know Elle Bradley.

Elle often *played* with her victims. To her, the business world was quite literally a cut throat one. She savoured the look of shock on a rival's face, after being lured into a luxurious sense of false security. On numerous occasions her victims had realised far too late that you need wings to be able to fly. However, as she watched her guests from a spy hole in the cockpit, she formulated no such plan, she was after all under strict instructions that no harm should befall them. Ordinarily, Elle wouldn't accept strict instructions from anyone, but this was different, these instructions came from very high up. Actually that was wrong, she smiled to herself, they didn't come from high up, they came from low down, from very low down, from the very bowels of Hell. She brushed down the front of her tight fitting business jacket and skirt to remove any creases, (not that any creases would dare appear in her clothing) and joined her guests.

'I apologise for keeping you waiting. I do hope Mr Becker has seen to your every need.'

Jenny noted a slightly fearful look cross Mr Becker's face, before it quickly disappeared.

'He's been the perfect host, thankyou.'

There was something about this woman she didn't trust. The look that Becker had given was not one of an employee who had upset a possible client and faced the admonishment of his boss. No, it was more the look of a servant who had spilt wine down the front of a tyrannical king. She'd have to keep her wits about her with this one, no more champagne for her.

'Before I explain why I've brought you here, would you care for anything? More champagne perhaps?'

Jenny wondered if the others had suspicions too. Their eager nods at the offer of more alcohol quickly dismissed this thought, she was on her own.

'Not for me thankyou,' she said, covering the top of her glass with her hand.

After the glasses were refilled, Jenny noted an extra magnum left on the side. Elle gave a flick of her eyes to her two employees, who immediately left for the cockpit.

'Right, I don't believe in beating around the bush, so here it is. I believe that the four of you are looking to purchase and develop a large expanse of desert land. To which end you intend to create a second Hell here on Earth.'

Death raised slightly in his seat.

'What do..'

Elle held out her hand to cut off his likely series

of questions and denials. 'Lets just say I have a contact. A high up contact.' She raised her eyes upward to give the impression of a Heavenly contact.

This carefully rehearsed misguidance bypassed the difficulty of lying to an Angel. Technically she had not lied. The interpretation of how it was received was the lie, and therefore nothing to do with her. Similar to a teenage girl when questioned by her parents. "Where have you been?" "Over Lisa's." The parents interpret this as two girls hanging out. The drink fuelled orgy that occurred whilst Lisa's parents were out is never mentioned so no lie is told. Thus the eternal bond of trust between parents and offspring is maintained.

'Now I understand you're on quite a tight schedule, so I've taken the liberty of making some advanced arrangements. I hope I'm not being too presumptuous. But, may I present to you Hell Two.'

As she said this Elle wheeled out a scaled down model of Hell on Earth from the rear compartment. Even Jenny had to admit that it was impressive, everything was in precise, minute detail, right down to a couple of Imps whipping a tortured soul.

'And where do you propose we situate this, er, you know, Hell?' The champagne was starting to go to Death's head.

'Right here. If you would care to look out of the window on the left.'

Below them was a colossal expanse of desert land, marked out at intervals with bright orange flags. The helicopter banked slightly, and headed straight for the centre.

'Welcome to Utah. The home of Hell on Earth.'

Chapter 16

The helicopter touched down near a typical worksite portable cabin; situated roughly in the centre of the large marked out area of the proposed Hell. The skill of the pilot was apparent in the soft landing, all the more remarkable for the absence of a large letter H to tell him where he should actually land. As the rotor blades whined to a stop Elle led them into the corrugated aluminium cabin. The interior's furnishings were far removed from any expectations that may have arisen from its outward appearance. This was not a workman's hut with plastic chairs and coffee stained grey metal filing cabinets. Inside it looked more like an upmarket coffee shop with long sofas, bright bold purple walls and dubious examples of modern art hanging from the walls. An air conditioning unit provided cool fresh air, in marked contrast to the sticky, dry, choking air of the surrounding desert. At the far end stood a long brushed steel boxed table, displayed on top of it was another slightly larger version of the scaled model of Hell. The far wall directly behind the model, was covered with artistic impressions of the various key structures.

Elle walked them over to the model, and gave them an ingratiating smile.

'Let's be frank about this, you're probably wondering why I've taken such an interest. Well quite simply, I'm a business woman. And this is a great business opportunity. The penal system is one of the most profitable areas in America and world wide, it generates billions of dollars each year. As I see it, Hell is an obvious expansion in this field. But I believe it could be so much more, the possibilities are endless. For example, I have acquired the tenders from several large companies for the disposal of toxic waste. Hell would be the perfect dumping ground. From what I can gather, the more unpleasant we can make it, the better. It is Hell after all. Quite simply, I'm in it for the money. Now that's all well and good, but what's in it for you I hear you say? Let's start with you, Norris isn't it?'

'Er, yes.' He was quite nervous at being picked out first.

'Unlike the others you are a mortal, a human. Therefore, you have human needs and they cost money. I will ensure that you are more than adequately provided for, for the remainder of your life. It would only be fair to share some of the wealth wouldn't it?'

'Well yes I suppose.'

'From what my intelligence tells me, you aspire to be a deep sea treasure hunter. So you'll need a boat right?'

'Yes.' His face lit up, suddenly the seduction of the money made his dreams attainable.

'As a goodwill gesture right here and now, I'm giving you the ownership papers to my own personal yacht.' Elle passed over a large manilla envelope to Norris.

He eagerly opened it, inside were the ownership papers (already in his name) and a picture of a stunning 40ft luxury yacht. It was the sort of yacht that famous celebrities and royals went missing from, later to be found by local fishermen, dead and bloated. He was sold.

Elle carefully watched his face. One down, three to go. Norris showed the others the photo of his yacht. She read the looks of anticipation, as each imagined what she had to offer them. She smiled to herself. They were like little children looking at her version of Father Christmas bestowing gifts. But she knew better, they were accepting sweets and being enticed into her car. Then she caught it, a look of suspicion on the Angel's face, she'd have to be careful with that one.

'Right, Death. What could I possibly have to offer you? One whose concerns are beyond the worldly domain. Well look before you at the creation of Hell Two. You were entrusted by your superiors to find a suitable location, that is all. You will return with not only a perfect location, but agreement from the owner, me, planning permission (she placed the documents on the table), and blueprints for construction (another document). Everything I would imagine you would need, not only to secure your job, but also promotion.'

Promotion. The word rang like a peal of heavenly bells in Death's ears. She was right, how could they possibly refuse to give him promotion after such a job well done. He was sold.

'Now before we move on to you two.' Elle looked directly at Reg and Jenny in turn. 'I'd like you to view some additions I believe will be beneficial.'

Elle pressed a small button on the side of the table. A compartment rose slowly from the table alongside the model of Hell, revealing a series of further constructions to the same scale.

'This is the public area of Hell; including shops, restaurants, hotels, and of course, the airport. We have named it Armageddon. We thought our little town should have a biblical name. I see your confusion. Why build a town here? The answer is simple; tourism. And that is what I have to offer you Jenny. If you look here at the section of the outer wall of Hell you will notice it's glass panelled.'

Jenny bent over to look. Elle waited briefly, then continued.

'Imagine the multitude of visitors each year, viewing for themselves the torment of Hell. What better moral instruction could there be? We are living in an age of television, live pictures from around the world. People don't want descriptions in books to tell them what is happening, they want to see it for themselves. And they can. People will see loved ones and friends suffering. What better way of showing them the error of their ways? The Bible is a dead format, this is the future, this is the way to convert people. And you Jenny will be the Angel who brought this lesson to the people. You will be the Angel who brought a new moralistic age; an age without sin. That is what I have to offer you.'

Jenny couldn't help herself, she was excited with the prospect. Not because she could prove everyone who thought she was a bit of a flake wrong; but she could actually see the benefits for humanity, the souls that would be saved. She bit her lip. She wanted it so much, but her instincts told her something was wrong. Elle could see that she hadn't fully won over Jenny like the others but she still had Reg to go. She figured a three to one vote should be enough and that Angel wasn't fully against her, she was just undecided.

Reg was full of anticipation. Norris had a boat, Death had a promotion, Jenny was the saviour of humanity, what would he get?

'Now to you Reg. There would obviously be no point in offering you wealth, big houses, or fast cars, because of your disdain for the capitalist way.'

Reg's heart sank. A little red sports car wouldn't be too capitalist, good honest workers would get a wage for making it.

'What can I possibly offer a man with so noble a conviction?'

He cheered up a bit. Let Norris have his boat. She was right, he was a man of higher purpose and integrity.

'Look at the town of Armageddon, what greater example of capitalist greed can there be? Well no, because you and ethics have even inspired me Reg. The largest capitalist companies in the world have all invested in this project, and I have made each and every one of them sign an agreement; an agreement to pay the workers of this town a fair wage for a fair day's work, well above the national average. They will be the best paid workers in their fields; from hotel maids to shop workers, all will praise the name of comrade Reg. And to ensure they never forget who is responsible for their well-being; a statue.'

Elle produced a small scale bronze statue and placed it in the middle of Armageddon. It was of Reg holding a flag and beckoning on a group of workers behind him; a dustbin man, a female cleaner with a mop and bucket, and a waiter carrying a tray, amongst them. He pulled up his trousers at the waistband with pride. He was sold.

Elle could see that her offers had clinched the deal. She saw no need to push the point.

'Well I'm sure you have a lot to discuss, so I'll leave you in private for a moment, to consult with each other. Should you wish to forward any of the plans to your employers there's a fax machine *et cetera* in the corner.'

Elle had no intention whatsoever of leaving them alone in private. The cabin was monitored more extensively with listening devices and hidden cameras than some reality television show. She quickly made her way to the helicopter where she could eavesdrop from the recipient computer. She placed a set of headphones on and leant back in her chair watching the screen closely. She placed Norris' voice immediately, not even needing the image to confirm his distinct accent.

'...hit the jackpot. I'm in agreement with Death. The sooner we sign the better.'

'I'm not so sure.' It was the Angel. She knew she'd be trouble. 'It all seems too good to be true, if you know what I mean.'

'Maybe it is, or maybe it's just plain good.' It was Death's turn. 'You think she's got some ulterior motive, well yes she has. She wants to make money out of this deal. And to be honest I don't see why she shouldn't. We've been commissioned to find a suitable location for Hell, we've found it, if there's a few perks so what. You've got to admit it's the best we've found so far.'

Jenny nodded her agreement. He had a point, it was a very tempting proposal.

'Got 'em,' said Elle to herself. One quick call and she'd rejoin them. She had the number on speed dial.

'They're going for it.' She hung up immediately after the short informative sentence. He'd know exactly what it meant. She didn't have time to chat, she had wanted to get back to them, and get everything signed. Besides, Bacchaus wasn't the sort of person you wanted to stay on the phone talking about the weather to. She returned to a group of smiling faces; only Jenny's grin wasn't as wide or, it appeared to Elle, as genuine.

'It's a deal,' said Death. 'Where do I sign? Or to use a more colloquial term to these parts, where do you want my John Hancock?'

It should be explained at this point, that the reference to John Hancock as an idiom for a signature, derives from the signing of the American Declaration of Independence. However, should you wish to avoid a mostly inaccurate history of this event, feel free to skip to the next chapter as what follows has little significance to either the plot, or the story in general.

As stated the use of John Hancock to signify a signature dates right back to the Declaration of Independence. The reason for this, is that the name

John Hancock is one of the few signatures clearly distinguishable upon the said document. This is not surprising, as in essence the Declaration at the time was an act of treason. Therefore it was tantamount to signing a confession, and as such, most of the signatories decided that their names should at least be a bit obscure. Until along came John Hancock. Historians have traditionally claimed this as evidence of his bold, fearless nature. Then in the 1970's historian Marshall Langhorn found new evidence to suggest that Hancock was in fact a bit thick. Young bright academics jumped on this breakthrough. Some argued that he believed the Declaration was a sponsorship form for George Washington to remain silent for the rest of the day, in aid of a prominent gout charity. Dismissing this, others claimed that he thought it was merely a petition and that if they got over a thousand signatures they would be free of all the tyranny that was going on. The latter theory received overwhelming support as it explained the scribbled obscure nature of many of the names, just like every other petition. Furthermore, the presence of the name John Hancock supported this theory. After all everyone knows it's a bogus name used to denote a signature.

Chapter 17

Archangel Michael was not a fretter, he did not fret. It was he that threw down Satan and his followers, he was not the type to fret. But if Death didn't call soon there would be threats. The last he'd heard, Death and his little group of... (He struggled for a word, he couldn't be too insulting he was Head Angel after all) Incompetents... they were heading for America. He'd read Death's file, and knew his penchant for the roulette wheel, and they were devilishly close to Vegas. Good job he wasn't susceptible to fretting.

Michael leant back in his chair and surveyed his desk, everything in its place, perfectly aligned, the two phones at perfect right angles to the computer screen and pens standing vertically out of their black plastic holder. It was the sort of pen holder that creative childrens' programmes make out of toilet roll and sticky backed plastic.

He was definitely more in control of his emotions these days, he was the absolute epitome of control. In his youth he'd been criticised for being too rash, a bit head strong, but the years had mellowed his personality. The pencil he'd been twiddling between his fingers snapped, and quickly joined the others in the waste paper basket positioned five inches from the end of the desk.

The Archangel pressed his thumb and index finger against the bridge of his nose and gave it a little massage. He'd had a busy day. Opening a new Hell was a logistical nightmare. It wasn't just about the relocating of souls, there was also the security aspect. If an evil soul escaped into the outside world it would be bad enough, but if a Demon did, it would be a disaster. He couldn't have evil denizens of the Underworld roaming around freely on their lunch break. Yet for Hell on Earth to function properly the Demons had to have their full powers. He'd tried thinking of alternatives but when it comes to eternal suffering and damnation no-one is quite as good as a Demon.

In the end Michael commissioned several, very costly, purpose built enchantments to keep the Demons and their destructive powers within the confines of Hell Two. Prices had certainly risen since the early days of the Abyss, but well, that's inflation for you.

That wasn't the end of his problems though. Hell on Earth was intended to be a temporary holding facility. Once Hades was reopened, all the sinners would have to be transferred back to the original Hell. The trouble was, Demons were notoriously difficult to evict.

Anyone who thinks getting the last guests in a house party to leave is hard, should try inviting a Demon along. They will try anything to stay, including chaining themselves to the toilet. If you think this is an exaggeration then watch the film *The Exorcist*. Look at the trouble those priests had and that was just one Demon and one little girl. Imagine if it was hundreds of Demons and a small town.

The solution had been surprisingly simple, but yet again costly. The expense arose because it involved lawyers. Lawyers were few and far between in the Heavenly Realm (the majority pen for the other side). A clause was written into the binding contract: Hell Two would only remain fully functional whilst a soul abided within its borders.

In essence once the sinners left, the Demons had to leave as well. Michael was pleased. Problem solved. Besides it added a bit of extra pomp to the ceremony; he could lead a procession with the first sinner to enter the new Hell. He always thought pomp was the best bit of pomp and ceremony. Once the first soul entered Hell Two it would be open and officially under the jurisdiction of the Demons.

There was nothing more he could do. Everything hinged on Death finding a suitable location. Good job he wasn't the type to fret.

A sharp double knock at his door broke his lack of fretting.

'Enter.'

Susan Pendridge duly entered, in her hand a stack of documents.

'See I told you not to worry, Death 221 has come through.'

'I wasn't worried.' The Archangel looked guiltily in the waste paper basket. 'What's he come up with then?'

'Everything. We've got full planning permission, complete blueprints for the brand new Hell and an excellent location.' She felt a glow of triumph, she'd backed Death and he'd come through for her with flying colours.

'So we're good to go?'

'Yes, thanks to Death 221, we've got everything we need right here.' She placed the documents on the desk (at a ever so slightly disjointed angle noted Michael).

'Really?'

'Yes. Well I haven't had a chance to do a proper background check on this...' She quickly flicked over the front page of the top document. 'Elle Bradley. She's the property owner.'

'Is she a mortal?'

'Oh yes.'

The Archangel flicked briefly through the collected documents, his eyebrows raised slightly with approval. Some of the proposals were quite ground breaking; Hell as a tourist location. How come he hadn't come across this Death 221 before, his talents were definitely being wasted, and Guardian Angel Jenny, the whole team in fact. Pendridge interrupted his thoughts.

'Shall I do a background check?'

'Oh no need I think. Time is of the essence. Sinners are queuing up.'

'If that's all?'

'Yes. Yes, and well done.'

Pendridge left the room leaving the Archangel to himself. As soon as the door closed behind her he reached down, slid open the side desk drawer and withdrew a packed folder. Big bold letters were written across the top; Construction Tenders. He had already put out a request for building tenders on the creation of Hell, and the replies had been numerous, they'd even had an offer from a ship building firm; Noah and sons. In the folder was his shortlist of three. Each needed a revaluation before a concrete offer could be given. He began scanning through the shortlist.

Pyramid Construction; a good solid company, their constructions certainly lasted. However, there was also a lot against them. They were known for building the roof first, a severe shortfall that was highlighted in the Ancient Egyptian project, plus the excessive labour costs (since slavery had been abolished).

Next Seamus O'Leary Construction, also known as O'Leary Construction, Seamus Building and Patio Ltd, S. O'Leary Driveways, and The O'Leary Brothers' Construction Company. Attached was a business card "Seamus Joseph O'Leary quality construction: As seen on T.V." Unfortunately the as seen on television referred to the consumer rights' programme; *Crooked Traders*. Besides which, Michael was pretty sure they were the same company that had built his extension, Seamus and Finnigan O'Leary Construction Specialists; the roof leaked and cracks had appeared after the second week. The only reason they'd got this far was because they were cheap and he was on a budget, but with many of the costs already bypassed with Death's efficiency (such as hiring an architect), he didn't need to cut too many corners.

He pulled out the final proposed tender; Jericho Construction Ltd. They were a long established company, and had tried hard to overcome a bad reputation they'd earned in their early days, and as such, had always had to keep their prices a bit lower than their competitors. Attached to the tender was a note from the company director. "Jericho Construction has long tried to maintain a reputation of quality workmanship. The problem of walls collapsing after the seventh blow of a ram's horn has now been fully rectified. The problem was not one of Jericho Construction's, but of our suppliers, who provided poor quality mortar; a supplier who is longer used by ourselves."

Michael leant forward, pressed his fingertips together, as if in silent prayer, his lower lip resting on the two index fingers. After his brief moment of contemplation, he pressed the intercom unit to communicate with his secretary.

'Moneypenny (it had been commented that Moneypenny only got the job because of the name). Can you contact Jericho Construction for me? Thank you.'

'Right away,' answered a deep baritone voice.

Michael quickly scanned over the plans. The project was of biblical proportions, quite literally. Well not literally in the sense that a second Hell being built on Earth is mentioned in the Bible, but literally in the sense that the proportions were biblical; they were measured in cubits. It was also quite large.

The Archangel sat assessing the time scale for the work that was to be undertaken. After careful consideration he surmised four to five hours should be ample time, but allowing for delays he set the deadline at six hours. After all the whole universe, with light, and plenty of other stuff, had been created in seven days, even allowing for a day off. Granted for this creation they were sub contracting but still six hours seemed fair. His mind wandered slightly when he thought of The Creation. Big Bang Theory, Michael chuckled to himself, the only thing created by a big bang was a lot of smoke and a large crater. The Heavenly Welcome Committee always had great fun teasing Big Bang theorists about it when they first arrived.

The intercom buzzed, Michael pressed a button opening the communication.

'Yes?'

'I've got Jericho Construction on line two for you, shall I patch them through?'

'Yes right away, thankyou Mr Moneypenny.'

Michael pressed the intercom button again and picked up the phone receiver.

'Ah, Tony how are things in the building game?'

Chapter 18

The Westland Lynx touched down smoothly next to the Volvo Estate. The four left the helicopter waving their goodbyes to Elle Bradley. They were in good spirits as they thought of the deal they'd just struck. Each of them had gained from the agreement. Reg hadn't even given a second thought to his imminent second death in a ball of fire and twisted helicopter metal. He'd been far too busy thinking of his statue. As the helicopter banked sharply away, they were left to consider their next move. For Death the next move was sleep, and from the look of the others there wouldn't be much in the way of complaint. It had been a long day and they were all suffering from pan dimensional lag. People often comment that death never sleeps, this of course is not true. Death was a great supporter of sleep, especially in his own bed. Unfortunately, his bed wasn't an option. Before he could go home he would have to drop Norris and Jenny off and get Reg registered in Heaven. It was far too much of an undertaking in his present state.

'Don't know about the rest of you, but I'm beat.'

The others agreed.

'Why don't we all just grab a few hours kip in the car, then drive over to the new Hell site tomorrow.'

No-one was in the mood to complain about this suggestion, sleeping in the car seemed like a good idea. Sleeping in the car always seems like a good idea when you're tired, (unless the car is in motion and you're the one driving, then it falls into the category of bad idea). It's not until the fresh light of morning that you ask yourself the question, 'what the hell was I thinking?'

For sleeping in the car there is a simple, yet strict procedure that must be adhered to. The first thirty minutes to an hour must be spent trying to get comfortable enough to actually sleep. This involves positioning your body in a reasonably comfortable position avoiding all protruding objects; such as steering wheels, hand brakes, and seat belts. It is then important that you wake approximately three to four hours into your sleep. This allows you to register that you're freezing cold, the position you thought was comfortable isn't, and you need to go to the toilet. At this point you should also take note that anybody else in the car with you is sleeping soundly, apparently in the lap of pure comfort and if possible snoring. The next thirty minutes should then be spent trying to get comfortable again and back to sleep, allowing the others to go through the same process you just did. Finally, upon waking, (just a little bit too early) you should find yourself with an extremely stiff neck, even more desperate for the toilet, and with sticky drool on your cheek. Thus allowing you to ask yourself, "what the hell was I thinking?" Thankfully the four companions followed these guidelines to the letter.

As the first light of the sun reached the car, (just bright enough to extinguish any hope of an extra hour's sleep) a shimmering figure appeared before them, with the strumming sound of a harp. His long white robe and feathery wings spread out full, distinguished him as an Angel.

'Behold, do not be afraid, I bring great tidings.'

'Yeah enough with the do not be afraids Gab. What's the message?' said Death grumpily.

'There is no need to cower, for I am...' said Angel Gabriel.

'Yeah, Angel of the Lord, I get it, we're not shepherds you know.'

'Oh.'

'It's always the same with this guy. All beholds and do not be afraids,' whispered Death to his companions.

'So you're not cowering then?'

'Come on Gab you know me, Death 221 Human Transition Department. We met at the reception to Matt and Verity's wedding.'

'Oh yeah, sorry. Didn't recognise you there. What about the others, they might be afraid?'

'That's Jenny, she's an Angel aswell, and Reg, technically he's a ghost.'

'What I'm a ghost?'

'Technically, yes, but don't worry about it you're registered. And Norris, he's a mortal but Jenny's his girlfriend so he kind of gets the whole Angel of the Lord thing.'

Both Norris and Jenny blushed at Death's nonchalant statement of their relationship status and deliberately avoided each others' eyes.

'Right, well I've got a message for you.' Angel Gabriel passed Death an envelope. 'I'll be off then, got another twenty of these to deliver.'

With the sound of a strumming harp the Angel disappeared. Death ripped open the envelope and pulled out a letter with gold leaf writing.

'What's it say?' asked Reg eagerly.

'Dear Death Third Class, Number 221, of the Human Transition Department. You are cordially invited to the grand opening ceremony of Hell on Earth, at twelve noon today. This is a formal occasion so full ceremonial attire is required. Oh great, it's a black robe and scythe affair.'

'What about us?' Reg tried to look over Death's shoulder but even on tipped toes it was a futile effort.

Death scanned down the letter.

'You're all invited to the reception after.'

'What! After all this we don't get to go to the opening?'

'Well they're probably restricted in numbers. Deaths have to go, we do a lot of work there remember. Besides the reception is the best bit anyway, it's where everyone gets a bit drunk. The formal side is boring. In the night, that's when the party starts.'

'Well it's just typical, we do all the work then all the posh nobs take the reward. No disrespect to you and your fellow Deaths of course, but the workers never get the credit. They just palm us off, oh you can go to the reception after. What they're really saying is you're not good enough for the actual ceremony.'

'Have you seen the itinerary? It's hours of speeches before the actual opening. Do you really want to go to that?'

'What listen to hours of bourgeoisie waffle? Not a chance.'

'So why are you complaining?'

Truthfully, Reg hated that sort of thing, pomp and ceremony made him feel very uncomfortable, it was just that he suffered from the human trait of worrying that his slice of cake was smaller than everyone elses'.

'Because, because. It's just typical that's all,' he added lamely.

Jenny leant over Death's shoulder, looking at the letter.

'Is anyone famous going? To cut the ribbon or however Hell's being opened.'

Death read down the page.

'Archangel Michael's cutting the ribbon, but Hell isn't officially open until the first sinner has entered. Someone called Gianni Colletto. I guess he must be some high profile criminal, Mafia or something.'

In fact, Gianni was in no way connected to any organised crime or any universally recognised crime by the law courts, at all. After much discussion the

Angelic Committee had decided this was a perfect opportunity to raise the profile of one of the lesser known sins. Everyone had sort of got the message about murder, stealing, that sort of thing, being wrong. Even adultery and false idol worship were commonly recognised, although not necessarily adhered to, but people generally got the message they were doing something wrong. Coveting however, had slipped through the net. Gianni had been the perfect choice, he coveted worse than anyone else in history, he committed covet after covet. All day long he would covet others possessions, wives, and cattle. Gianni was a serial coveter and now it was time for him to pay.

'We actually should get a move on if we're going to get there in time,' said Death, checking his pocket watch. 'I'll just phone one of the boys to bring my cloak and scythe along with them.'

To most people *one of the boys* would be John from accounting, or an old school friend called Tom, or similar, but for Death it was the Four Horsemen of Everyday Life (Negligence, Accidental Misadventure, Casual Violence and Suicide). He pulled out his mobile phone from an inner pocket of his suit jacket.

'Can't get a decent signal. Anyone else got a signal?' he asked, after swinging his phone around at arms length in several directions.

Jenny and Norris both checked their mobiles, shaking heads revealed that they had the same problem. It was at this point Reg realised he'd left his mobile in work, he'd never get it back now. Death jumped up onto the bonnet of the car keeping a constant vigil on the signal bar of his phone and slowly made his way up onto the roof. Each footstep gave a crumpling metallic sound which made Norris inwardly cringe as his battered car took the brunt of Death's endeavours.

'Ah ha! Got it.'

Death quickly dialled the number.

'Hey Negligence it's Death here.'

'Hey buddy.'

'I was wondering if you could do me a favour, could you possibly bring my cloak and scythe to the opening?'

'Can't sorry fella. Me and Oops have been banned from Hell until it's all open.'

'What you and Oops?'

'Yer, apparently we were disrupting the building schedule, with the number of accidents. Kept telling them it's my job but would they listen?'

'No way. Well can you tell Casual Violence to bring them then.'

'No problemo.'

'Cheers. You still going to the reception though right?'

'Of course, ever known me to miss a party.'

'Cool see you there.'

'See ya buddy.'

Death liked Negligence, he was always so laid back about things. He jumped off the roof and slipped into the driver's seat.

'Everybody in. We'll make a quick jump and then get freshened up for the opening.'

'Or just the reception,' grumbled Reg, as he climbed into the back.

Even though it was a relatively short distance to Hell, Death decided to make a pan dimensional jump to save time, (which was handy because the journey itself would have doubtlessly been boring and nobody would really be bothered with a rehash of the same old stuff). Had he chosen to drive, the journey could have been summed up in five words, sand, sun, road, tedious and hot. Not even a game of *I spy* would have made it remotely interesting.

'Er, before we make the pan dimensional jump, can I just ask a question? There's something I don't get,' Norris asked.

'Shoot away,' replied Death with a sigh.

'Well, it doesn't make sense. The world revolves on a fixed axis right, you know the equatorial line and all that. So surely we can only travel along that fixed axis, yet we've been able to skip from one place to another randomly. Basically, we've been able to travel sideways not just in the direction the world is spinning. How?'

Norris was the sort of person that pointed out a possible disastrous flaw in the plot when it was already too late to do anything about it. He was the sort of person that didn't think to question the blueprints when something could be done about it, oh no, he waited until the construction was almost complete. Luckily Death had the answer.

'It's quite simple really, the dimensions we jump between are on a slightly different axis', so we zig zag our way there. A bit like a sailing boat that wants to cut across the wind to change direction. It's basically tacking.'

'Oh, I see,' said Norris, with a confused look on his face.

'But you'll know all about tacking being a deep sea treasure hunter,' said Death, without a hint of sarcasm in his voice. He believed that sometimes sarcasm was best enjoyed privately.

Death sped forward and broke hard. The jump was made with the usual lack of flashing lights and fanfare. The car appeared before a large boldly written sign. *Welcome to Hell. Home of Sinners. Twinned with Naples.* At the bottom a digital counter informed them "population 0." The powers that be had decided that digital was the most efficient way to keep up with what was expected to be an ever increasing population.

They looked upon the site with awe. Where there had once been barren desert, there now stood a fully constructed city.

'Is this the same place?' asked Norris.

'Oh yes,' said Death. 'The Celestial Realm is legendarily expeditious. Look at the Universe; all created in a week, with enough time spare to pull out the patio furniture, sit back, and admire your handy work. Let's find a hotel where we can freshen up a bit before the ceremony.'

They headed past the sign down Judas Avenue, into the district of Armageddon (the tourist area of Hell). The road was lined with cheap tacky gift shops, bars, and restaurants, all vying for the forthcoming tourist trade. Two fast food restaurants dominated the street. One claimed it provided "one hell'uv a burger," the other "a heavenly hamburger in the midst of Hell." A compromise had obviously been met between the two rival chains, although the managers stood in the windows eyeing each other suspiciously.

The avenue led them to Sodom and Gomorrah Plaza, at its far end stood the Hellview Hotel, its stone fascia infested with numerous gargoyles. The impressively grand entrance to the hotel wasn't what caught the travellers' attention though. In the centre of the plaza surrounded by bench seats, stood a gleaming bronze statue.

'It's my statue!' exclaimed Reg. 'Stop the car! stop the car!'

Death pulled up outside the hotel and all four got out.

'I can't believe it, a statue of me, Reg Hallsworth.' He read the inscription on the stone plinth supporting the statue. 'Reg Hallsworth; champion of the workers.' He took a few steps back and looked up at the statue again. 'Although, it doesn't really look like me does it? I mean that figure's a bit dumpy looking, a bit short and fat, I know I'm holding a few extra pounds but come on. And I know I'm getting a bit thin on top but he's bald!'

'Well I think it's artistic licence, they've captured your noble essence, it's more about your spirit,' said Jenny.

Reg pulled up his trousers in his customary gesture.

'Yes you're right. It is more about capturing a political ideology.'

Death couldn't help thinking how many such statues he'd seen being pulled down over the years; usually by disgruntled mobs, who'd decided that they weren't so keen on that political ideology after all.

'We may as well get a couple of rooms here.' Death pointed over his shoulder at the Hellview Hotel.

Jenny eyed the stone steps leading up to what promised to be an extremely lavish hotel. As tempting as it seemed, she suffered from an angelic sense of prudence.

'It looks expensive.'

'Don't worry we'll get the cheapest rooms.'

Death bounded up the steps with enthusiasm, leaving the others trailing behind. This was more like it, although not completely averse to roughing it, he definitely preferred a touch of luxury. A set of revolving doors swished smoothly giving him access to a cool and excessively marble reception area. The receptionist broke off her conversation with the concierge to greet them.

'Good day to you, how may I be of assistance?'

'Hello. We're looking for four rooms, adjacent if possible.' Death gave a quick glance at Jenny and sighed. 'The cheapest available please.'

'The cheapest rooms we have, are in the west wing. They have a full panoramic view of Hell.'

'The cheapest rooms are the ones with the view?' queried Norris from behind Death.

'Yes sir.' The receptionist turned her attention to Norris. 'Although we do have a number available at a slightly higher price with a more obscured view. It's hardly a view at all, you have to go out onto the balcony before you see anything.'

Norris was confused.

'But surely rooms with a view are more desirable?'

'Not when the view is Hell sir.'

'But people are coming here to see Hell.'

'Yes sir, but it works a bit like a graveyard. People are quite willing to visit them, place flowers on loved ones' graves *et cetera*, but far less keen to sleep in one.'

'Oh yer, I see your point.' Norris turned to Death. 'I don't want one with a view.'

'Me neither,' said Reg shuddering as he remembered his recent experience of Hell.

Death looked at the others.

'We'll take four partial view rooms, and not go out onto the balcony. Agreed?'

The others nodded in compliance. With a sharp flick of her wrist the receptionist hit a brass bell on the desk, summoning a young porter in a red suit jacket that looked tailor made for someone else.

'That's rooms 104 through to 108. Edward take our guests to their rooms please.'

'Right this way please,' said Edward, leading them to a mirrored elevator.

Chapter 19

Norris lay on the hotel bed. Each of them had their own separate rooms; Jenny's was tantalisingly situated next to his own room, with Death and Reg's rooms across the corridor. As soon as he had entered the pristine room the bed had called out to him. Although largely regarded as inanimate objects, beds have the power to *call out* and entice you to join them with some sort of psychic ability; an ability shared with refrigerators and food cupboards during a diet. Often you'll hear people say *my bed's calling,* thinking they are just tired. Little do they realise that their bed *is* actually calling them. The bed's ability to communicate with mankind can perhaps be attributed with the closeness of their relationship. There's nothing quite like sleeping in your own bed. A relationship that is particularly acute amongst the student population. However, sometimes the relationship goes bad, commonly referred to as insomnia.

Norris did not have insomnia, he just couldn't sleep. It was his thoughts that kept him awake, most of them revolving around Jenny, but not all of them. The past few days had been quite traumatic. He chuckled to himself. Quitting your job, building a tree house and painting yourself green, not the signs of a sane person. He still liked the idea of being a deep sea treasure hunter, but he couldn't deny it, he'd definitely lost his mind back then. Luckily he was perfectly sane now. Reality had returned. He was laying in a hotel bed which overlooked Hell on Earth, waiting for the after-ceremony party. A party he was attending with his friends; Death, the ghost of the man he'd killed, and an Angel. Yep, he'd definitely regained his sanity.

Jenny couldn't sleep. Her thoughts kept her awake, most of them revolving around Norris, but not all of them. She had a nagging doubt that something was wrong. She felt like they'd been somehow manipulated into the construction of a new Hell. It was like a jigsaw where the pieces didn't quite fit. No that was wrong. The problem was the pieces did fit, all too well. It was just she had a feeling that it wasn't the picture she'd expected. Somehow the picture on the box of two fluffy kittens had been replaced with two snarling rottweilers.

Reg couldn't sleep. His thoughts kept him awake, most of them revolving around his statue, no wait all of them revolving around his statue. It wasn't vanity that made him so preoccupied. It was more about pride. A statue of him; Reg Hallsworth. His ageing Aunt Maude had always warned the young Reginald that *pride came before a fall*. Contrary to her sagely advice, in his experience a stumble and trip usually came before a fall. Pride rarely played a part in instigating a fall. If it did have a role, it was generally to be dented after the fall. Safe in the knowledge that he was unlikely to suffer a fall, he decided to go for a walk, and maybe take another look at his statue. Besides, he had half an hour before meeting Jenny and Norris in the hotel cafe bar. They'd agreed to meet there whilst Death was attending the opening ceremony. There was little else to do, none of the amusement rides were open yet.

On his way to the foyer Reg decided to call on Death. He gave two loud raps on Death's door. No answer. Reg tried again. Listening for a response he realised that the shower was in full blast, he'd catch up with him later. It's funny he thought, when knocking on Death's door you don't expect to be greeted by perfumed steam billowing through the cracks, or for that matter the sound of a monotone rendition of *Bohemian Rhapsody*.

Sodom and Gommorah Plaza was largely deserted. The tourist town of Armageddon wasn't open for business yet. Reg wandered around the paved outskirts of the Plaza, secretly hoping the occasional worker that passed by would recognise him. None of them did. Maybe if he stood a bit closer to the statue, somebody would make the connection. Nobody did. After half an hour Reg gave up. Looking back at the sculpture it dawned on him why nobody recognised him. It portrayed a short, tubby man with stubby legs, and a slightly bald patch. It was nothing like him.

Reg found Jenny and Norris sitting at a round polished oak table in the hotel's cafe, and slid into a free chair next to them.

'I wondered where you'd got to.' Norris turned to Jenny, her attention seemed elsewhere. 'Reg is here.'

'Oh I'll have a hot chocolate, thanks.'

'Reg. Not the waiter.'

Jenny finally looked up. 'What? Oh yes sorry, hi Reg.'

'What's up Jen? You've been in a world of your own since we got here.'

It was as if a dam suddenly burst in Jenny's thoughts, all her concerns came flooding out.

'It's just I don't quite trust all this. I feel like we're being manipulated somehow. It's just a feeling I've got. Take Elle, her offer, it all seems too good to be true. And how did she know what we were doing, she's a mortal, she shouldn't have known any of this.'

'She had a tip off remember, from high up she said.' Norris pointed upwards conspiratorially.

'But no-one would have tipped her off from the Heavenly realm. What if her tip off came from down below instead?' As she said it, all her scattered thoughts came together. 'That's it! She was tipped off from someone in Hell. Someone in Hell wants all this to happen!' she turned to Reg. 'Why didn't they break the strike in Hell? They just let it go on.'

'When workers unite they are a powerful force.'

'Really?'

'Well,' Reg hesitated. 'To be honest I wondered that myself. The boss down there didn't even want to negotiate.'

'Satan you mean?' asked Norris.

'No, I thought that, but apparently he's not in charge of the day to day running. I never got the name of the guy in charge. Although, now you mention it, from what I heard he was the sort you didn't cross. The sort that would have no trouble breaking a strike. They kept calling him a bad 'un, which must mean he was pretty tough considering who called him that.'

Jenny spoke her thoughts out loud. 'A bad 'un, that kind of sounds familiar.'

'Well it is a common phrase.'

'Yeah, I suppose. Anyway, I think it's looking like someone in Hell wanted a new Hell to be built on Earth and that can't be a good thing. I just don't see why they'd want it. What is there to gain from it?'

The three sat in silence for a moment, each attempting to provide a possible solution to Jenny's question.

'Maybe they wanted a sort of holiday from the other Hell, it's kind of depressing. This way they get to walk around the Earth,' offered Reg.

Jenny's face dropped as if every muscle in her face suddenly decided to take a quick nap.

'Oh no.'

Reg and Norris looked at each other fearfully.

'Jen, what's up?' asked Norris.

'Don't you see we're giving Demons the power to walk the Earth! Demonic powers are restricted when they're here on Earth but this gives them that power back.'

'What like a Judgement Day?'

'The last days when the dead rise from the grave,' quoted Reg knowledgeably.

Norris was quite impressed. 'Is that written in the Bible?'

'Well no it's from er, Ghostbusters. But they do say something about it being in Revelations.'

Jenny eyes gave a quick flicker of recognition. Leaning down she pulled out her heavy brass bound Bible from her handbag and began flicking through the pages.

'Revelations. Revelations. What did they call the boss in Hell again?'

'A bad 'un.'

'It's not a bad 'un, it's Abaddon! I knew I'd heard the name.'

Jenny pushed the Bible in front of them and slammed her index finger down on the relevant section.

'Look here, chapter thirteen. I saw a star which had fallen down to the Earth, and it was given the key to the Abyss. The star opened the Abyss, and smoke poured out of it, like smoke from a large furnace; the sunlight and air were darkened by the smoke from the Abyss. Locusts came down out of the smoke upon Earth and they were given the power...'

'Locusts don't seem so bad,' interrupted Norris.

'This is a prophecy, it's kind of cryptic. Lets just say the star is some Fallen Angel, the Abyss is obviously Hell, and the locusts are Demons from Hell, not so good now is it? Here look!' Jenny skipped a few paragraphs. 'They have a king ruling over them, who is the Angel in charge of the Abyss. His name in Hebrew is Abaddon. See a bad 'un,

Abaddon! He's got other names, Demons always do, it's to hide their deeds, but he's also known as Apollyon which translates from the Greek as The Destroyer! Get the picture, we've got trouble. Basically, Abaddon is trying to kick start the Apocalypse.'

Reg was seriously worried. Not the kind of worry that you get when you think you haven't done enough revision for an exam, but the kind of worry you get when you think your actions may have caused the total destruction of mankind.

'Surely this is just a prophecy, it won't necessarily come true will it?' he asked hopefully.

'That's the whole problem with prophecies, they tend to come true. That's why there's a committee in charge of restricting them. It's called a self-fulfilling prophecy. Once the words have been spoken they have a habit of dictating events. It's like when someone visits a fortune teller and gets told their destiny lies with someone in a red coat. Next person they see in a red coat they chat up thinking it's their destiny to be with them. One thing leads to another and they end up with that person, and the prophecy comes true. It would be fine if people just stuck to the small things but oh no, they always want to prophecise the end of the world. Take Abaddon, would he have planned all this if he hadn't read about it first? Anyway, even if this isn't the Apocalypse, we're still giving Demons the power to roam the world. As soon as the first soul enters Hell on Earth the Demons will have access.'

Reg was getting desperate, there was even a statue telling everyone it was his fault.

'They'll be restricted to Hell though won't they?'

'Possibly, but I think that's where that...' she wanted to say bitch but she was an Angel so she spelt it out instead 'B.i.t.c.h Elle Bradley comes into it. She gave us those oh so perfect blueprints;

blueprints that, if I'm not mistaken, will have included a gap in the boundaries of Hell Two. A secret little gap that will allow the Demons to have access to the rest of the world.'

Jenny paused dramatically as if waiting for some music to burst in; dum dum da. Instead Norris spoke up.

'I think maybe we should stop them opening Hell.'

'I think you might be right,' said Jenny pulling out her mobile phone, and frantically pressing numbers. 'I'll call Death, he's there, he'll be able to stop them.'

'Hey this is Death. I'm unavailable at the moment, but if you leave your name and number, I'll get back to you as soon as I can.'

'No answer! Death er, this is Jenny, Angel Jenny. Er, you've got to stop them opening Hell, er Hell Two that is, not the other Hell. Oh dear, I never know what to say on these things. Er. We've been tricked I'll explain when we see you. It's Abaddon, he's a bad 'un. I know that doesn't make sense to you right now. Er, just stop Hell opening, or call me. Thanks.'

Norris sprang out of his seat.

'Come on. He's probably got his phone switched off for the ceremony. We'd better drive over there.'

The three ran to the car, Norris jumped into the front driver's seat, Jenny took the front passenger and for once Reg jumped into the back without any fuss. After a brief fumble with the keys, Norris turned the ignition. Nothing happened. He tried again, the car gave two wheezing chugs, then started. Then stopped with a hiss and a small puff of smoke. Norris hit the steering wheel hard, the car didn't even respond to his sudden outburst of violence.

'It's had it! What are we going to do now?'

'I'll try Death again.'

'Er we could walk,' said Reg. Jenny and Norris turned to face him. 'Well it's only five minutes away. And by my watch the grand opening doesn't start for another twenty minutes.'

'Oh, yer of course,' said Jenny, a slight blush touching her cheeks.

In defence of Norris and Jenny's panic, they hadn't had that much experience at stopping apocalyptic events, so naturally they thought they were on a tight schedule. Their knowledge on the subject, (mostly film based) consisted of the hero stopping the timer on the bomb with a second to spare. They hadn't considered the possibility that they'd had time to finish their cappuccinos, casually saunter over to the event, and still have time to save the day.

Heedless of the apparent amount of available time, the three headed for the opening ceremony at a brisk jog, (which due to the magnitude of events was quite understandable). As a result of the jog and the numerous stops for Reg 'to catch his breath a minute' they arrived at the ceremony seven minutes later. Much to his chagrin Reg's physical fitness and athletic prowess had followed him to the afterlife.

On the left-hand side of the main entrance to Hell a platform had been constructed. On it stood a long table where the dignitaries and speakers sat. The majority of the table was occupied by representatives of the Heavenly Body, although a number representatives from Hell sat on the far right-hand side. Between the immortal enemies, strategically positioned, were a few departmental heads from the realm of Death.

The Deaths provided a supposed neutral barrier between the two. The Death Realm Charter states that all Deaths must adhere to a neutral position between good and evil. The reality however, usually finds Death slightly biased to the side of good. It has been argued that due to the option between good and purest evil, it is only natural that Deaths will inherently side towards good, as anyone would. It has also been commented that Heaven pays Deaths' wages.

Needless to say, there was a degree of tension on the top table. It was similar to breakfast at a guest house, where a certain couple had kept the rest of the guests awake all night, with a display of drunken exuberance that filtered through the walls. Smiles and pleasant nods disguising the tension that hid in the outraged whispers between the various offended factions.

In front of the platform sat row upon row of guests, the seating arrangements mirrored that of the front table, although, the majority of the "Hell Section" had empty seats. They were the sort to answer yes to the R.S.V.P then deliberately not turn up. If the atmosphere was strained on the table, it was beyond breaking point amongst the crowd of onlookers. On the table, the representatives were politicians, and as such, were used to dealing with each other. The assembled audience had no such dealings. If the top table was like breakfast at a guest house, then this was breakfast at the Middle East peace talks; where a couple of delegates had blown up half the guest house and the others were holding their children hostage in the shared television lounge. The tension in the air was so thick it almost obscured vision.

Norris and Jenny looked across at the assembled throng. Reg just looked at his feet, puffing heavily after his exertion.

'Where's Death?' asked Norris.

Sitting in front of them were hundreds of Deaths, all wearing the traditional ceremonial robes, with their scythes propped up next to them. It should be noted that Norris was looking for a particular Death; Death 221, and not just Death in general, of which there were quite a few to chose from. Jenny understood this.

'I can't tell.'

From behind all the Deaths looked the same. It was like trying to spot a nephew in the crowd of a televised football match; sure he'd told you he'd be wearing his teams jersey but so were half of the assembled mass. As hopeless as it was you still looked.

'I think that's him. Over there!' Jenny pointed.

From behind, at a distance, with a hooded cloak pulled up, most heads look the same. The odds, on Jenny actually picking that particular head, were remarkable. They rushed over at tapped Death on the shoulder. As he turned around they realised their mistake; remarkable but wrong.

'Oh sorry I thought you were someone else,' said Jenny.

He turned back around, muttering something about all Deaths looking the same.

'Over there, that's him!' Norris waved. 'Psst. Death,' he whispered. 'Death. Death.'

'He can't hear you,' said Jenny, avoiding the excruciating pun about Death being deaf.

'Death!' said Norris, just short of shouting.

Thirty or so Deaths all turned around, none of them the one they were looking for, including the one Norris indicated. He tried a different tack.

'Sorry, erm, I'm looking for Death 221 of the Human Transition Department.'

As the others turned back round a rosy cheeked Death nodded his head towards them.

'Wait a sec.'

He turned to another Death several seats to his left.

'Death.'

'What?'

'Where's Death sitting?'

'Who?'

'You know, Death.'

'Oh right yeah. He's down at the front, three rows back.'

'There you go,' said the rosy cheeked Death.

'Er, thanks,' said Norris.

Reg now able to breathe again, looked at the row upon row of Deaths between them and Death.

'We'll never get through.'

Jenny looked over at the Hell Section. The empty seats had created a crooked pathway through to the front. It was a maze of Demons, and they liked nothing better than to pull the wings off Angels. She gave a big sigh.

'I think there might be a way through.'

Norris followed Jenny's gaze.

'Oh no, you can't mean...'

'I'm afraid so. It's the only way.'

Jenny led them over to the Hell Section.

'Okay, we need to stay focused. If we don't go too near any Demons we should be able to pass through undetected. Oh, and pull an evil face, like you're really angry.'

The three *saviours of the day* cautiously wove their way through the assembled Demons. The going was slow but they found they were able to make their way to the front without having to go too close to any Demons. They were almost half way through when Norris looked at his watch.

'We're running out of time, we've got to go quicker.'

At that moment, they heard a voice behind them.

'Hey you.'

Turning slowly, cold shivers running down their backs they were confronted by an Imp.

'Reg? What you do here?'

Reg gave a sigh of relief as he turned to see the grinning face of Ugrat.

'Shhh. Keep your voice down.'

Ugrat looked suspiciously at Jenny.

'Me thinks that's an Angel. Angels steal children Imps if they good. Take them away in night and eats them for breakfast.'

Reg didn't have time to explain that it was an urban myth that Imp parents used, to ensure their offspring behaved badly when relatives visited.

'It's okay she's with me. She won't eat any baby Imps.'

'You sure?'

'I promise.'

'Okay then.'

'Comrade Ugrat, I need a favour. We need to get to the front, can you help us?'

'Ugrat help, Reg.'

'Thanks.'

'For fifty thousand pounds.'

'I er, don't have any money.'

'Make little joke, make you laugh yes. Course Ugrat help, me sure you part Imp.'

With Ugrat leading the party they were able to pass much closer to Demons and were soon at the front. Reg turned to Ugrat.

'Thank you comrade. How's the strike going?'

'Strike over.'

'What Hell's open again? They gave in?'

'Hell open. Boss not give in though. Imps get bored, too many of nice things happen.'

'Oh. Well thanks again.'

With that Ugrat turned and made his way back to his seat.

'That confirms it then,' said Jenny. 'With Hell reopen there's no need for all this. Unless Abaddon is planning something.'

'What are you doing here?' Death had seen them approaching and had made his way over to them.

With relief they all grabbed and hugged Death.

'I've only been gone a couple of hours.'

'We've got to stop the opening. There's no time

to explain now but it's the Demon Abaddon, he's planned all this. There's going to be an Apocalypse.' Jenny quickly explained, her words tumbling over each other.

'You sure?'

'Yes!' said all three in unison.

'Okay, this way.' Death led them towards the front table and the entrance to Hell at a brisk pace. Their brisk walk turned into a run as they saw Archangel Michael lead the others at the table towards the gateway to Hell.

'Quickly, they are opening Hell,' said Jenny, increasing the speed.

The four were brought to a sudden stop by a huge, bulky security guard who suddenly stepped in their way.

'And where do you think you lot are off to?'

'I need to speak to Archangel Michael, right now. We've got to stop them opening Hell, if they do it'll cause an Apocalypse,' explained Death.

'It can wait till after the opening. I'm sure he'll listen to your concerns then.'

He embodied the image of the over-muscled and dim-witted security guard. In other circumstances, Death would have found comfort in the fact that there was a basis in the stereotype, and that maybe it wasn't such a narrow minded view after all. Unfortunately, this wasn't an *other circumstances* moment it was a *this circumstance* moment. So Death tried to explain himself slowly.

'We-need-to-stop-Hell-from-opening-right-now. If-we-don't-then-it-will-be-the-end-of-mankind. So-we-need-to-get-through-now-or-it-will-be-too-late.'

'I'm-sure-it-can-wait,' replied the security guard adopting Death's speech pattern.

'No it can't wait!'

'No need to lose your temper sir.'

Nobody noticed Jenny quietly slip away during

the discussion and head back towards the Hell Section.

Norris looked at the procession to Hell's gate. Michael had been given an oversized pair of gold scissors and was moving towards the purple ribbon that spanned the gigantic gates.

'We need to hurry,' Norris whispered urgently.

As Archangel Michael cut through the ribbon, a cacophony erupted from the Demons watching. He wasn't expecting such an enthusiastic response, funny he thought, as he looked across.

Jenny stood in front of the section containing the most evil denizens of the Underworld, her Angel wings spread out revealing her full Heavenly self. The gathered Demons were in uproar at her appearance in their section.

'ANGELS RULE, DEMONS er, ARE um, RUBBISH!' Jenny taunted the already jeering Demons. Her announcement fuelled the frenzied abuse, the Demons reacting like an angry mob of football hooligans surged forward. Security guards appeared from everywhere, bustling Jenny away and trying to nullify the explosive situation.

The security guard in front of Death lifted his hand to his ear piece.

'You lot, wait here.'

As the guard ran off, Death duly waited. It lasted the half second it took his body to catch up with his brain. Norris and Reg dashed after him. People are often heard commenting on a quick death being better than a slow death; although few spouting these wise words have ever actually experienced death, quick, slow, or otherwise. In this case though they were actually right, a speedy Death was quite handy.

Gianni made his way to Hell, his eyes fixed firmly on the golden scissors in the Archangel's hand. What a lovely pair of scissors he thought, what I could do if I had a pair of scissors like that.

I want those scissors, he doesn't deserve them, I do. Oh well, once a coveter always a coveter. His thoughts were interrupted suddenly with a whirl of black cloth and a hard thump.

Death pulled Gianni down with a super league tackle, Reg quickly piling on top of the flaying limbs, effectively pinning the sinner to the spot. Norris stood over them. To his right Jenny had arrived and was explaining the situation to Michael. Norris looked up at the gateway to Hell, Gianni was less than a foot away. Stopped just in time, he thought, now that's how it's supposed to be, saving the world with a second to spare. His only comment on this was 'humpph,' as a bulky security guard came crashing down on him.

Chapter 20

It had taken hours for the four of them to fully explain the situation. During this time most of the gathered guests had slowly filtered away once they realised that Hell wasn't going to be opened on Earth after all, and any chance of a reception party had been dismissed. Their faces showed shock and disapproval, like guests at a wedding where the bride didn't show; faces that hid the excitement of having a topic of gossip for numerous years to come. The four unlikely saviours sat shellshocked in the cafe bar attached to the hotel. They had spoken little on their journey back; each had taken time to reflect on the events. Archangel Michael had initially been angry, but his disposition soon changed when their story unfolded. By the end they were being universally heralded as heroes.

As Norris leaned over his coffee, his mood was subdued. This is it then, he figured, end of the adventure. Everyone would go back to their own lives, or deaths, back to their, or at least his own ordinary hum drum lives. Even this was a denial of what was bothering him, he couldn't even admit it to himself. He loved Jenny. There, he'd said it or at least thought it. He'd probably never see her again.

'Hey,' Death broke into Norris' thoughts. 'Why the glum face?'

'Oh you know, it's just...'

'Yer I know what you thinking.' (although he didn't) 'You thought we'd be going to the reception. I was looking forward to the party aswell.'

'No it's not that.'

'Really? Oh. It was going to be an awesome party mind.'

'It's all over isn't it. We're not going to see each

other anymore. You guys will probably still hang out and stuff, but I don't belong in your world. You guys, well you're immortal and I'm a mortal, I've got a mortal life.'

'Hey don't worry about that, I'm sure you'll be joining us sooner than you think.'

Death had never quite mastered the art of cheering someone up, his words of comfort always seemed to have a double meaning.

'Oh great.'

Jenny decided to take over.

'I'll still see you, I'm your Guardian Angel after all,' she hesitated, maybe he didn't want to see her. 'If you want, that is?' she ventured.

Norris took in her words. He felt elated, she wanted to see him. Okay so it was in an official capacity, he would've preferred it if she'd said she couldn't live without him or something like that, but it was a start, something to build on.

'I'd really like that.'

'Really?'

'Yes, of course.'

Jenny almost sprang out of her chair with joy.

'Maybe we could go bowling again?'

Norris couldn't believe it she was asking him out.

'That would be great,' he paused, he'd been an idiot, she did genuinely like him. 'Er look, I've been really stupid. What I said before, I was wrong. Of course I believe you all exist. It was just a shock that's all and well I'm glad we all got to do this.'

'To comrades!' Reg lifted his coffee cup in a toast.

Cups clinked together as they all joined in the toast.

'That reminds me.' Jenny pulled out a form from her bag and passed it to Norris. 'It's to say that you'll deny that any of this has actually happened. Michael was quite firm about it, he doesn't want any of this getting out. You will need to sign the bottom.'

'Do I need to use blood or anything?'

'No a pen will be fine,' said Jenny giggling, he was so cute.

As Norris was signing the document, the hotel's concierge strode over to their table.

'Mr Hallsworth, there is a call for you. You can take it in the foyer.'

'For me?' queried Reg.

'Yes sir.'

'Better get used to it Reggie boy,' said Death. 'You're famous now. You'll be in demand.'

'Famous?'

'Yep, we did save the world you know. There will be interviews, photo shoots, the papers are probably writing up our story as we speak.'

Death's comment was particularly insightful. As Reg followed the concierge to the foyer, the editor of the high brow Angelic Times was putting the finishing touches to the front page copy. He leant back and examined the bold headline; "Calls for more stringent safety measures as Apocalypse is narrowly avoided." Further down the street the Daily Saint was running a similar story. A large photograph of Jenny with her wings spread wide, standing in front of the Demon audience (the angled picture highlighting her cleavage) dominated the front page. The caption beneath claiming "Angel reveals all to Demon mass as chaos breaks out at grand opening. Full story inside."

The concierge pointed to a phone, the receiver resting on the reception desk, then furtively looked across to a solitary figure sitting on one of the numerous chairs scattered around the foyer. Reg followed his gaze to the man, his head buried deeply into a newspaper. Funny he thought, the hotel seemed surprisingly deserted, even the reception desk was unmanned. Perhaps everyone had gone home. With Hell not opening the whole area would hold little purpose, certainly there would be no need for such a grand hotel. He turned to ask the concierge what the future held for Armageddon, but he was already quickly scurrying out of the room. Probably quite busy thought Reg, with all the staff leaving. He reached across and picked up the receiver, a low humming sound instantly told him that the line was dead.

Death leant back in his chair. 'Actually why are we drinking coffee, it should be champagne. We are heroes and we have just saved the world. If that's not cause for celebration, what is?'

'Why not?' agreed Jenny. 'We did win, didn't we?'

'Yep we certainly did. They've sealed the gates to Hell Two so no stray souls can get in and inadvertently give Demons access to it. Crisis over, drinking begins.'

Death waved his hand to get the attention of the concierge who had just reappeared. The concierge took one look across and disappeared out of the cafe bar.

'Funny bugger, I only wanted to order some champers,' muttered Death.

Jenny looked over her shoulder and shrugged. 'Maybe he's busy.'

'I thought that Abaddon fella would have put up more of a fight,' said Norris. 'What with all the planning he must have done. I guess he's just a coward.'

Death knew Abaddon by reputation and one thing he wasn't was cowardly, unless it suited his purposes of course. He turned to Jenny.

'They did seal up the entrance properly didn't they?'

'Yes, Michael saw to it himself. Why you don't think he'd still try something?'

'No I guess not.'

Jenny suddenly looked worried.

'You know the entrance to the new Hell was one way. Abaddon must have had a secret entrance. Otherwise he'd just be stuck within the borders. For his plan to work, he'd have to be able to leave Hell Two freely and still have all his powers. He provided the blueprints through that Bradley women, remember?'

'Yer.'

'Did anyone seal that secret entrance?'

It was Death's turn to look worried.

'I don't think so. There's no need to panic.' His face told a different story. 'The Human Transition Department are carefully monitoring all souls until Hell Two is demolished. I'd better give them a ring though, just to warn them.'

'Er, you said your department was monitoring all souls?' asked Norris.

'Yes of course.'

'Does that include Reg? He's a soul isn't he?'

It took the briefest of moments for Norris' bombshell statement to fully sink in, before all three dived out of their chairs. They reached the foyer in seconds. Reg was nowhere to be seen, the only evidence that anyone had been there was a crumpled newspaper lying on the floor. They quickly pushed their way through the revolving door and out onto Sodom and Gomorrah Plaza. In front of them standing over a now opened manhole stood Bacchaus, with Reg slung unconscious over his shoulder.

Throughout the centuries Bacchaus had taken on many forms and many names; he was Exterminans, he was Apollyon the Destroyer, and most famously he was Abaddon. His fame had spread down through the ages with numerous guest appearances in works of literature: Revelations, Bunyan's Pilgrims Progress, Milton's Paradise

Regained, the Dead Sea Scrolls and the list goes on. He even appeared in the Dr Who spin-off Torchwood (although he wasn't too pleased with his portrayal in that one). At this moment, in his human form, he went by the name of Victor Bacchaus. Even in human form the Demon was a daunting figure, six foot plus of rippling muscle. His silver grey hair and angled chiselled features, only served to highlight the coldness of his heart. His dark black eyes watched them cooly as they approached.

'So I see you've discovered my backup plan, most inconvenient.'

'You can't get away with this,' declared Jenny, as they drew nearer.

Bacchaus sneered. 'Oh but I can, and will.'

As is typical with most megalomaniacs, (to which society he belonged) Bacchaus relished the idea of talking about his cunning and malicious deeds. He never realised his fundamental error of wasting time talking about his crime instead of finishing it. It is often at this moment that the hero will take his opportunity to get out of the sticky situation (usually imminent death) and overcome his nemesis. Unfortunately, the said heroes in this case never realised his mistake either, so they just listened.

'Do your simple minds have any idea of the work that has gone into my little project? A burst water pipe and incompetent workmen, a broken latch on a briefcase and a gust of wind, all planned meticulously; just to get a staunch trade unionist in Hell. Planting a subliminal idea of creating Hell on Earth into his feeble mind, oh yes that was my idea too. And yes you must have guessed by now, a secret entrance in and out of Hell. Maybe it will fulfil that apocalyptic prophecy, I cannot say. It will however, give me unprecedented power on this mortal Earth. And you think you can stop me? Go on just try and I will crush you, like a beetle under my foot.'

Norris warily eyed Bacchaus' powerful figure. He had to admit he did present a convincing argument. However he'd always been told to stand up to bullies, talk tough and they'll back down, that was the school yard rules and Norris knew how to talk tough.

'Oh yer, you and who's army?'

Bacchaus sneered again.

'I'm glad you asked. Me and my army,' said the Demon, raising his hands up and giving a guttural chant.

The ground beneath their feet began to shake throwing them off balance. With a loud crack a large fissure appeared, Reg's statue went crashing into the gaping hole. Snapping and creaking echoed throughout the plaza as more cracks appeared. A burst water pipe sent water high into the air, and then cascading down the half submerged statue. As the crevasses widened, shadowy figures with twisted bodies and grotesquely tormented faces slowly began to emerge, smoke billowing around them as they rose. Norris cursed himself, he should have gone with *my dad's bigger than yours*. Although come to think of it that one probably wouldn't have been such a good idea either.

'Behold my army, my locus horde.'

With a final sneer and a snort, Bacchaus jumped down the manhole, Reg still slung over the Demon's shoulder. Jenny quickly pulled out her mobile phone, her message was brief.

'I need your help, Sodom and Gomorrah Plaza. Hurry.'

One of the Demon horde rose from the ground just in front of Jenny and grabbed at her ankle. With a scream she jumped back and launched her phone at it. The phone shattered as it hit its target between the eyes, with a groan her assailant fell back into the fissure.

'They haven't got their full strength, their powers are weakened,' she informed the others.

'Yer, but I think we're slightly outnumbered,' said Norris, pulling her back towards the hotel.

Already over a hundred Demons filled the plaza and more were rising from the numerous cracks. With a blinding flash several nearby fiends were thrown back covering their eyes. When the burst of light subsided standing between them and the horde stood three lone Angels.

'Having a spot of bother Jen?' asked Angel Katie. 'Lucky really we were just round the corner, checking to see if any Demons were still hovering around after the ceremony.'

'Katie! Am I glad to see you.'

Death coughed suggestively at Jenny, and flicked his eyes at Katie.

'Oh sorry, er, Death this is Katie from Angel Force Three. Katie this is Death 221 of the Human Transition Department.'

'I've heard about your exploits stopping the Apocalypse,' said Katie.

'Oh it was nothing.' Death decided not to mention the nasty bruise he'd received to his knee. 'I just acted like anyone would, I didn't have time to think about it. Now if some people want to call me a hero, fine, but I was just doing my job. But I'm sure you know all about that.'

'Oh you'd be surprised, not everyone acts like you did.'

'I guess that's just the kind of guy I am. Look after all this is over, why don't you let me take you out to lunch? I know a great little tapas bar.'

'That would be nice. Look I've got to go, Demon horde to fight and all that, but get Jen to give you my number.'

'Definitely.'

Katie glanced back at Death as she joined her

companions; Aimee and Lily. Cute she thought.

The three Vengeance Angels stood shoulder to shoulder. Angel Aimee took a slight step forward towards the now hesitant Demon army.

'Demon horde go back to the Abyss whence you came or face the wrath of Angel Force Three.'

The evil denizens of the Underworld glanced nervously amongst themselves. They'd heard of Angel Force Three's terrifying reputation, but on the other hand they did have the numbers. Although mathematics isn't a Demon strong point it was quite easy to figure out they had roughly a hundred to one advantage. The odds seemed good.

'Oh yer, make us,' said one particularly brave Demon, standing in the front.

'Okay.'

Aimee leapt forward and kicked the lower half of his jaw clean off. Damn, he thought, I should have gone with *my dad's bigger than yours,* and collapsed in a crumpled heap. With a front flip Aimee landed gracefully in the middle of several of the Underworld's finest; a spinning roundhouse kick sending them flying backwards.

Lily took Aimee's lead, pulling her laptop bag off her shoulder she jumped forward. Swinging the bag around her head, she charged into the Demons unfortunate enough to stand in her way. She soon cleared a space around her wide enough to, well, swing a laptop bag. One wily Demon managed to duck under her swing and threw a punch at her. In one swift blur of movement Lily pulled out her laptop, opened it, and caught the punch inside, slamming the lid shut. The Demon yelled in pain as his hand got crushed. She wrenched the computer free and struck him in the nose with it. As he fell down comatose she casually slipped the laptop back into its bag. Lily really was quite good with computers.

Even the most cunning Demons who stayed at

the back soon found there was no hiding from Angel Force Three, as Katie rained down fire and brimstone from her position on the hotel steps. Angel Aimee whistled to get Katie's attention, with a tilt of her head she indicated the burst water pipe. A knowing smile crossed Katie's face and she gave an understanding nod. Taking a deep breath she raised her hand to the sky. Then with a flick of her wrist sent a lightning bolt slamming into the middle of the fountain. The Demons standing in the large puddle that had formed around the burst pipe, barely had time to realise their mistake before they were fried.

The lightning explosion seemed to signify the end of round one, as both Demons and Vengeance Angels simultaneously stopped to take a breather. The eerie silence that descended as both sides cautiously watched each other was abruptly broken by a tinny, melodic, and most of all, embarrassingly cheesy ring tone. Angel Aimee looked slightly abashed as she answered.

'Hi mum. Look I'm a bit busy at the moment. Yes I know I'm always too busy. Yes. Yes I know you weren't too busy for me. Okay, yes okay I'll pick up a pint of milk on the way home. Yes Lily's fine, look I really have to go. Oh okay, love you too mum.'

The brief truce ended as swiftly as it began. Thirty or so Demons came rushing through the foyer behind Death, Jenny, Norris and Katie, forcing them down the steps towards Aimee and Lily.

'They sneaked behind us,' Katie informed Aimee, as the two groups joined.

Within seconds the group found themselves completely surrounded by an ever increasing army. The six of them stood back to back in a small circle surrounding the manhole as even more Demons poured into the plaza, slowly encroaching on the gap between them.

'I'm afraid I don't think we can win this one,' said Aimee. 'There's just too many of them.'

'But we have got to stop Abaddon,' implored Jenny.

'Yes you're right,' agreed Aimee. 'You three go, stop Abaddon. We'll hold them off for as long as we can.'

'But...'

'Just go. Now.'

Jenny knew it was pointless arguing, they had to disrupt Abaddon's plans at all costs. She gave Angel Force Three a brief nod and disappeared down the manhole, Death and Norris close behind her.

Chapter 21

Reg became aware of a jostling, bumping motion, and the sound of... water, splashing water. He concentrated on the sound. After a short while he realised the splashes coincided with each jerky bump. He wasn't quite ready to open his eyes yet, as flashes of memory flew in front of his closed eyes. A newspaper being thrown on the floor. A large man walking towards him. No wait it wasn't a man, his eyes they changed. Then nothing just a sense of falling. Reg became conscious. He was being carried. Carried by a Demon. Abaddon. It must be Abaddon. Before he cautiously opened his eyes he allowed himself one last thought; bugger!

Norris finally reached the bottom rung of the iron ladder and joined Jenny and Death. Each step of the way down, as the sounds of the fighting above slowly became muffled, he told himself he wasn't afraid of the dark. By the time he'd reached the bottom, he was convinced he wasn't afraid of the dark. He had no fear of the dark whatsoever, he was afraid of what was in the dark! Under normal circumstances he could rely on rationality; Demons and monsters don't exist, unfortunately in this case, rational thought worked against him. Demons did exist and he was actually looking for one, in the dark! The biggest baddest Demon at that, but at least he wasn't afraid of the dark. As he looked around the stone clad sewer he noticed that it wasn't that dark at all. At regular intervals the passage was dimly lit by luminous lights held in metal cages high up on the curved walls. The blue green lighting left long stretches of passageway hidden in sinister shadow. Great he thought, now I've got to overcome my fear of sinister shadows. Jenny reached out and took hold of his hand; sometimes Angels are afraid of sinister shadows too. Death was standing in a few inches of mostly water, rolling up his trouser legs. In a display of confidence he'd jumped the last few feet and now was regretting the decision.

'Great,' he muttered. 'This suit is ruined. Why did it have to be a sewer?'

'Which way?' asked Jenny.

'The new Hell is that way,' said Death looking up and flicking his head. His socks were ruined too and they were his favourite pair.

The three headed off quickly but cautiously in pursuit. As they travelled down the sewer other outlets joined the passage they walked. Jenny finally stopped after passing one such outlet.

'Are you sure we're going in the right direction?'

'Yep this passage is heading straight towards Hell Two, Abaddon must have come this way.'

Her concerns pacified, Jenny continued. A few hundred yards further on Jenny stopped again. 'Which way now?'

In front of them the passage split into two, both apparently heading in the general direction of Hell.

When Gandalf had faced a similar problem in the Mines of Moria, he confidently pointed to the correct way because the air smelled less foul that way. His sagely advise that "if in doubt... always follow your nose" however, held little sway with the three companions who had no intention of using their noses for anything in the sewers of Hell, particularly smelling. Instead they went for the far less astute advice often pronounced in horror films.

'We'll split up,' said Death. 'I'll take the right, you guys take the left.'

Jenny looked at Death, concern in her Angel eyes.

'Good luck,' she said solemnly, and led Norris down the left hand passage.

Reg had little idea why Abaddon was carrying him over his shoulder through what appeared to be a sewer, but he decided now was not the best time to ask. Suddenly, Abaddon stopped and slung him unceremoniously off his shoulder. Reg hit the floor with a splash. It took all of his will power not to show any reaction to the pain and the unpleasant feeling of liquid effluent seeping through his clothing and running down his face. He listened, keeping his eyes tightly shut, as Abaddon took a few steps away. Then he carefully opened one eye. He was in a large cavern-like structure, behind him the round circular opening of the sewer spewed out its waste. The Demon stood in front of a large iron gate, in his hand he held a set of keys bound to an oversized metal ring. Taking one of the keys he unlocked a thick chain binding the gates together. With a clinking, grating sound he slowly pulled the chain free and cast it aside. Something told Reg that time was running out, if he was going to make his escape it would have to be now. He quickly formulated a plan. It was a simple plan. Reg jumped up and ran away as fast as he could.

Sometimes simple plans are by far the best plans; on this occassion, this wasn't the case. The fundamental flaw in this plan was Abaddon could run faster than Reg. He got barely a hundred feet away before the Demon caught up with him. Grasping him round the neck the Demon lifted him cleanly off the floor. Although still in human form Abaddon's height meant Reg's legs dangled a couple of feet short of the ground. Abaddon knew he could easily put Reg back into his comatose state, but he enjoyed the terror that was coursing through his victim's veins, so he dragged him back kicking and screaming.

Jenny and Norris heard Reg's yells echoing down the passage ahead. They exchanged glances and sprinted towards the noise. Death also heard the yells. Realising he'd taken the wrong route quickly turned around and followed the passage the others had taken. Jenny and Norris reached the cavern first. In front of them standing at the gate stood Abaddon, his left hand pinning a struggling Reg to the solid ironwork of the gate, his right hand releasing the lock with the key. With a light that instantly lit up the dim cavern, Jenny revealed her true Angelic countenance. Her wings unfolded and spread wide, and her pale skin took on a soft shimmering glow.

'Demon Abaddon as a duly elected member of the Heavenly Host, I command you to release the soul of Reginald Hallsworth, whereupon you will return unto the Abyss whence you came.'

She'd stolen that last bit from Angel Aimee but thought it sounded good. She held little hope that Abaddon would comply with her demands but, well, it was worth trying. The Demon slowly turned to face them.

'I don't think so.'

This was a problem for Jenny; regardless of the odds she'd kind of hoped he'd go along with it, and now she was stuck with what to do next. Should she just charge at him, fists flying? She wasn't sure. She'd never really had to start a fight before.

'Erm okay.'

Luckily for Jenny, Abaddon solved her dilemma and went into one of his, now swiftly becoming predictable, megalomaniacal speeches.

'What you thought that was it?' he laughed. 'Just say you're a naughty Demon and off I'd trot. Or did you think you could fight me and win? You an incompetent Guardian Angel and him, a sales rep, who cowers when his boss yells.'

'Deep sea treasure hunter,' whispered Norris.

'And...' The Demon looked around. 'Where is the other one, Death?'

'He's on his way.'

'Are you sure? Maybe he's come to his senses and right now is making his way to safety? The Deaths are not known for their heroics you know. Do I see doubt in your eyes? You know you can't trust him don't you?'

Death reached the end of the passageway when he heard his name being spoken. He hesitated for a bit, as the temptation of hearing what people had to say about him took over. He had to admit, the Demon had a point, running away seemed like a good idea. Then Jenny spoke.

'Ha! You don't know anything about us. We're friends...' She looked at Reg 'We're comrades. And that is something you will never know about or understand. Right now it doesn't matter if we can win or not, you've got our friend and we're going to fight.'

Death quietly slipped into the cavern while everyone's attention was drawn away. His silent entrance was almost disrupted as he stumbled on a pile of rubble lying discarded to the side. Reaching down he picked up the offending item; half a house brick. Might come in handy, he thought.

For the first time the Demon wasn't so confident with his chances. Sure what he'd said was true, but then again his powers were weak here on Earth. Even if he took on his Demonic form there'd still be a chance of defeat. But there again. Abaddon burst into his Demonic form; muscles split through his human skin, scaly wings stretched out and his face took on his otherworldly self. His cold black eyes studied his opponents, his thin lips curled back revealing his splintered yellow fangs.

'Very well. A fight it is.'

Death knew a thing or two about fighting. He had studied most martial arts; unfortunately not much beyond first or second belt, he'd never really been committed enough. If he was honest with himself the only reason he'd got that far was because most of his opponents had been under the age of twelve. That didn't matter, in his line of work he'd learnt one sure thing; the best fighting technique, martial arts or otherwise, was to sneak up from behind and hit them with something heavy. In this technique he was black belt. So it was that Death edged his way behind Abaddon, feeling the weight of the half house brick he'd picked up along the way. Admittedly he regretted not bringing his scythe, but the brick had been an opportune find.

The Demon had survived for thousands of years in his various guises; Bacchaus, Apollyon, and of course Abaddon, and you don't survive in the Underworld without learning a thing or two about sneaky bastards. It had been Jenny and Norris that had given it away. Only a slight glance to his right, but it was enough. A quick step to the side left Death's blow wide of its mark. In response the Demon struck Death in the lower back with his knee. Already off balance from his attack Death went sprawling forward, crashing face first onto the floor. Reg kicked the Demon hard in the shin, as Jenny and Norris rushed towards the melee.

Surprisingly, Reg's attack had little effect. With a twisting motion Abaddon threw the short man. His arms and legs swinging wildly, Reg slammed into Norris sending them both to the ground in a heap. Jenny kicked at the Demon's groin, but he was too quick and blocked her blow. Abaddon slammed his forearm down on the Angel's shoulder forcing her to her knees with a scream of pain.

Norris struggled to free himself from Reg, who groaned in semiconsciousness. He knew he had to help Jenny, as a flurry of blows rained down on the crown of her head. Slowly and deliberately the Demon lifted Jenny to her feet, her head swaying from side to side. He looked at Norris, a malicious grin spread across his face, then he struck. With a clenched fist the Demon punched Jenny in the chest with a sickening crunch. Her helpless body flew backwards and hit the wall next to Norris. The stone behind the Angel's head cracked, sending debris to the floor with her limp body.

Norris crawled next to her and sat stunned, cradling the Angel's crumpled form. Her fragile body showed no sign of life. No breath passed her lips and no flicker of recognition showed on her face as he called her name. Norris gently laid Jenny's body down on the floor. Tears streamed down his face, but they weren't just tears of anguish, they were also tears of anger. He'd never felt anger like this, an intense burning rage rose up in Norris. He turned towards Abaddon.

'You've killed her!' he screamed.

'Let's finish this mortal.'

The Demon strode towards Norris, casually kicking Death who was slowly rising from his prone position. Norris wanted revenge, he wanted to hit the Demon, hit him with anything he could get his hands on. Reaching out his hand grasped the handle of Jenny's handbag. He leapt up swinging the handbag wildly, left and right. Abaddon casually stepped backwards out of range each time Norris moved forward, leaving the swinging blows wide of their mark.

Out of the corner of his eye the Demon noticed both Reg and Death were slowly rising. He didn't hear the click as the bag's latch broke or see the heavy brass bound Bible come shooting out. He did feel the blow as the corner of the brass clasp made contact with his temple. The mortal had stopped his furious attack, it was his turn to strike. He tried to raise his fist, but nothing happened. Something felt wrong. Abaddon tried to move but his whole body felt like it was seeping away. His knees hit the floor. Realisation dawned on him.

'No!' Abaddon managed a last scream before his ethereal presence was torn back to Hell.

The three watched as the body of Abaddon slowly crumbled to dust and washed away with the sewer water. Norris broke out of his stunned daze.

'Jenny!' he exclaimed, turning and running back to her.

Norris gently held her head and smoothed back a strand of hair that had fallen across her face. Death casually walked over to Norris and put his hand on his shoulder.

'She's not dead you know,' said Death as a smile broke on the corner of his mouth.

'What do you mean?' Norris turned his head sharply. 'Are you sure?'

'Well I have had some experience in that sort of thing.'

As if in response to Death's statement, Jenny's eyes flickered open and she gave a little cough. Norris gave a choke pulling back his tears, a wide smile spread freely on his face.

'She's not dead?' questioned Reg peering round Death.

'What do you think the *im* in immortal stands for?' said Death.

Norris looked up at Death, a touch of irritation showing on his face.

'You let me think she was dead.'

'Well you were doing so well, I didn't want to spoil your flow.' Death was now openly laughing. 'You want to watch that temper of yours.'

Norris joined in Death's laughter. Jenny opened her eyes fully to the sight of the boys all laughing.

'Did we win?'

'Yep. You should have seen Norris, standing over you, took out Abaddon with a mighty blow. Killed him stone dead,' said Reg, tapping Norris on the back.

'Well not exactly killing him,' said Death.

Reg looked behind him. 'What do you mean? He's still alive?'

'Don't worry, he won't be coming back. But it's that whole immortal thing again. Norris killed his Earthly body. Abaddon the Demon still exists. He has been banished though.'

'What that's it? After all this he gets banished. That's like giving some mass murderer community service work and a hefty fine. It's rubbish!'

'Hey don't blame me, I don't make the rules.'

'Banished,' grumbled Reg, his hands flapping at his sides. 'It's not like he even had a particularly agonising death.'

'Come on let's get back to the surface,' suggested Death, ignoring Reg's indignation.

Norris helped Jenny onto her feet, she wobbled slightly, perhaps a little bit over dramatically. Death gave her a puzzled look. In return she gave him a stare that spoke volumes, it said; shut up and don't say a word.

'Let me help you,' said Norris, putting his arm around her for support.

The four walked towards the passage, Jenny firmly in Norris' grasp. At that moment Aimee burst into the cavern, Lily and Katie close behind.

'Is everyone okay? Where's Abaddon?'

'Banished,' said Reg walking straight past them, kicking idly at the water around his feet.

'What about the Demon Horde?' asked Jenny.

'Oh, Michael and some other Angels turned up. They're mopping up the last of them now. Sorry we couldn't get here quicker.'

The three Vengeance Angels looked battered, their clothes torn and their bodies displaying bruises, scratches and cuts.

'No problem, we had Norris and his handbag,' said Death.

'Handbag?' asked Jenny turning to Norris as the enlarged party followed Reg back up the sewer.

'Er yeah. I attacked him with your bag. Your Bible flew out and hit him in the head. That's how he got killed, I mean er, banished.'

'Well that just goes to show, there's nothing more powerful than the word of God!'

'Especially when it's bound in solid brass,' muttered Death.

Epilogue

It was Reg's first day in Heaven. As he strolled to the coffee shop to meet Death, he studied everything around him. Heaven wasn't all that different from life on Earth, he mused. The difference wasn't in your surroundings, it was in the way you felt. Being in Heaven was like being in love, everything around you was the same but somehow it felt better. Put simply, you were happy, and everybody else was happy, Heaven was definitely a happy place. As he approached the coffee shop he could see Death sitting outside.

'Hey Reggie boy.'

'Death.'

'So how do you like Heaven?'

'Its good, really good. Haven't quite worked out what I'm going to do here yet though.'

'Well I might be able to help you with that. Remember you wanted to become an Angel?'

'Yes,' said Reg excitedly.

'Well I've pulled a few strings, you start this semester.'

Reg gave Death a hug.

'Thank you comrade, that's amazing.'

Death felt a bit awkward, he really wasn't too comfortable with the whole hugging thing. He put up with Reg's display though, most souls were a bit *huggy* when they first arrived in Heaven. It usually took them a few days to adjust.

'Well I did promise and it was quite easy for a Death of my standing.'

'You got your job back then?'

'Much better than that. I've been promoted. The youngest ever Head of Department, I got plagues. You are now looking at Death Second Class,

Number 221, Head of Plagues.'

'Head of Plagues doesn't sound too pleasant. But I'm sure it's one of the most important departments,' Reg quickly added, not wanting to offend Death.

Death wasn't offended and laughed.

'Actually it's one of the cushiest jobs in the profession. Plagues are few and far between these days. Nothing dramatic ever happens in that department. I get to just sit around and wait for the pay packet to arrive. I think they gave me the job just to keep me quiet. There's been a lot of publicity surrounding recent events, and I think they just wanted to keep me onside.'

Death pushed the Daily Saint newspaper across the table towards Reg. The front page was dominated by the heading: Angel Force Three Vanquish Demon Horde. Full story inside. Pages 2-6. Reg quickly flicked through the story.

'There's no mention of us.'

'Yes there is.'

Death leant over and turned to the relevant page.

'Here look, on page five. The Vengeance Angels were assisted by Death 221, Angel Jenny, Reginald Hallsworth (a recent soul in Heaven), and by Norris Beachley (a mortal). The four lent a helping hand when one of the Demons, who can't be mentioned here for legal purposes, tried to escape the Angels' wrath.'

'What? That's it, two lines.'

'Like I said they're trying to play it down.'

'After all we did, banishing Abaddon. Saving the world.'

'Reg I was there remember. You didn't do that much. You just kicked him in the shin. It was a good kick though. I bet he's got a nasty bruise.'

Death and Reg burst out laughing.

'Okay,' said Reg, tears of laughter running down

his face. 'I admit it, I didn't do that much. But it was a team effort, comrades together. What I did, was a diversionary tactic.'

Reg spent the rest of his first day in Heaven chatting to Death. Not once did he think of calling for strike action, because quite frankly, for once there was nothing to strike over.

****

The Demon Bacchaus stood in front of the Fires of Damnation, casually leaning against a long flat shovel. Had his plan succeeded it may have been different, but it hadn't. Satan had not been pleased. "Acting on his own without informing the Lord of Darkness was bad enough...but failing! He'd brought shame on the entire Realm of Hades."

He had instantly been demoted to the lowest and most menial job in the Underworld. Bacchaus straightened up and wiped his brow. Oh well back to work. As far as punishments went it could've been a lot worse. Besides he'd rise again. It's hard to keep a good Demon down. Or is it hard to keep a bad Demon down? It's hard to keep a Demon good at being bad down.

Bacchaus scooped up another pile of Dragon manure and fed the flames.

****

Deputy Hal Roberts walked through the door of the small sheriff's office, and took a sip of his polystyrene wrapped coffee. Only one other officer was inside.

'Morning Hal,' greeted Officer Meyrick, over the yells from the holding cells.

'She's still at it I see.'

'Ain't shut up all night. How long we gotta hold her here Hal?'

'Your guess is as good as mine. I'm just doing what that FBI fella says.'

'What she done anyhow?'

'FBI holding her on tax evasion, some guy Becker gave them enough to hold her on.' Hal leant in close and whispered conspiratorially. 'But from what I heard they is waiting for a new law to be passed, special for her like.'

'What's that?'

'Conspiracy to cause an Apocalypse.'

'Reckon she ain't going anywhere but the mental institution if you ask me. Been saying crazy stuff all night, all Demons and Angels stuff.'

Both officers leant across and looked at the prisoner.

'You can't hold me!' shouted Elle Bradley. 'I haven't done anything wrong. I'm not the criminal here. I've been framed by that bitch Angel. And him... he, he stole my boat that's what he did. He stole my boat!'

****

Of course, the world isn't a predominantly blue orange, its a planet. A planet that we call Earth, and on one particularly blue bit of this predominantly blue planet a boat rocked back and forth with a lazy swell.

Norris the deep sea treasure hunter stood on the deck of his luxury yacht and watched the sun rise on the horizon. Maybe he'd actually look for treasure today. That was the beauty of being your own boss; the word *maybe* often arose in your working week. Maybe, he thought. He lifted the hatch and descended the narrow steps (not too narrow this was a big boat) to the sleeping quarters, a glass of freshly squeezed orange juice in his hand. Quietly laying the glass down on the side cabinet, he looked across to the bed. Lying there in peaceful slumber was his girlfriend. She was everything he'd ever dreamed of. She was perfect in every way. After all, she was an Angel.

Coming Soon...

The Eleventh Plague

On Thursday, 4th September, 1400bc (give or take a couple of years) the ancient Egyptians suffered the first of ten hideous plagues. Eventually, after suffering boils, the death of their first born, and of course frogs, they let Moses and his people go. Just as well really, because waiting to be unleashed upon them was the worst plague mankind would ever know, to some minds even worse than the frogs.

The Eleventh Plague was carefully stored away where it would be safe and beyond the wit of even the most cunning thief. Basically, in a clearly marked jar, on the top shelf, out of the reach of wandering hands. There it stayed for over two millennium, but now it's gone. Believed to have been stolen by the mysterious (and obviously terrorist) group, the Galileists, the plague must be retrieved before it can be unleashed upon an unsuspecting world. Unfortunately for Death 221, the responsibility lies firmly with him. He really should have read the small print on his job contract. His only chance (and mankind's) is to reassemble the team, stop the Galileists, and bring back the Eleventh Plague before its too late.

www.ingramcontent.com/pod-product-compliance
Lightning Source LLC
Chambersburg PA
CBHW071600030726
47593CB00001BA/249

* 9 7 8 0 9 9 2 9 8 0 3 0 6 *